BY CHRISTY ANGELLE BAUMAN, PHD

Her Rites
The Sexually Healthy Woman
Theology of the Womb
A Brave Lament (with Andrew Bauman)

Her Rites

Her Rites

A Sacred Journey for the Mind, Body, and Soul

CHRISTY ANGELLE BAUMAN, PhD

CONVERGENT
NEW YORK

Published in the United States by Convergent Books, an imprint of Random House, a division of Penguin Random House LLC, New York.

Convergent Books is a registered trademark and the Convergent colophon is a trademark of Penguin Random House LLC.

Hardcover ISBN 978-0-593-72790-4
Ebook ISBN 978-0-593-72791-1

Rites illustrations by Kinsey Aleksi copyright © 2024 by Kinsey Aleksi and are used by permission of the artist.

Printed in the United States of America on acid-free paper

convergentbooks.com

9 8 7 6 5 4 3 2 1

First Edition

Book design by Diane Hobbing

For Selah, Rosemarie, Orielle, Piper,
Katriel, and Evie—the force,
and every female generation to come.

Contents

Her Rites Marking Guides

Creation Marking Guides

Intuition Marking Guides

Legacy Marking Guides

HER RITES

Everbearing

Under the rib cage of every woman,
a heart pumps blood throughout the body, making her a living
  creature.
Lay your head against her chest, and you will hear the song of
  her lifeblood.

Deeply nestled in a woman's pelvic floor,
her organs' pulse creates the most healing sound;
It is the echo resounding in the conch shell,
Lay your ear to her belly, and you will recognize the sound of the
  ocean's womb.

The woman's body offers an exquisite understanding of her rites:

She is both powerful and powerless in the same space.
The female story is a mystery, portraying the life-death-life cycle
  over her lifetime,
proclaiming that she is everbearing.

Her rite is that she belongs to herself first.

Introduction

Why Her Rites?

Your best self is your integrated self. An integrated woman is a rooted and whole woman; *she belongs to no one but herself.* In my work as a therapist, I say this to every client when she comes to me with questions about finding wholeness, fulfillment, or satisfaction. A self-aware woman must embrace all of herself: past, present, and future, physical and emotional. Self-awareness invites integration, and integration is the doorway to freedom. Sadly, too many women have a fractured knowledge of themselves. They are not living from a holistic, or integrated, self. My female clients tell me the same thing over and over: *I am not free.* Whether this is her body, or her mind, freedom is the goal. For many women, their spirituality has been taken captive, and they are no longer their own. This sense of not knowing herself, of being a woman who cannot find herself—her whole self— underlies a woman's disintegration.

Among thousands of conversations highlighting the female story, I learned to identify the concrete steps that equip women to draw back together the many aspects of themselves and their fractured stories. Together, we discovered tasks that helped them find their voices, awaken to their sexuality, and deepen their spirituality. A pathway to living intact and free. Vitally, I developed for my clients rites of passage and meaning making that gave new understanding to the moments in life when they become most disintegrated, leading them to wholeness. This is often through an intentional moment or rite of passage, integrating story work and body work.

A rite of passage is a ceremony to mark the gains and losses in life, but first we must discern what we have gained and lost, which is commonly done in story work. Rites of passage and rituals have existed for millennia. For example, in 2021, *The Journal of Black Psychology* did an extensive study of Dipo, which is a historical rite of passage among the Krobo people in the eastern region of Ghana. This rite assists pubescent girls as they transition into adulthood by inviting them to contemplate their morality, physicality, social skills, and sexuality. Women who underwent Dipo in puberty had better personal outcomes over their lifespan than the girls who did not. This study and other research have demonstrated that when girls know how to make meaning out of life situations, they maintain well-being throughout womanhood. What I have seen with my clients is that **it's never too late to make meaning—** that the rituals we do today can help draw out the significance of past life stages and transitions. The rites I will teach you in this book will help you embrace change and celebrate gains, losses, and grief with intentionality.

We all experience loss. As women, our losses may include the loss of sexual innocence, outgrowing simplistic faith, moving away from a beloved home, the loss of friendship, a rupture in church or community, betrayal, a hysterectomy or mastectomy, the stepping down of someone in leadership, or the death of a loved one. Grief and outrage are essential responses to loss. How we engage our grief informs how we make meaning of our lives. These losses can negatively impact our mental health, and we have learned that resiliency is critical to surviving and thriving after difficult experiences. Research has shown that meaning making is essential to becoming resilient. If we do not acknowledge and find meaning in our experiences, we cannot grow from them, nor can we heal from adverse experiences.

In *Her Rites,* I will equip you with knowledge and guide you in drawing out the spiritual and emotional significance of the most common female rites of passage that you have lived through or will experience in the future: birthright, initiation, exile, creation, intuition, and legacy. Whether you go through these rites alone or with a few close friends—which I hope you'll consider— you will newly discover and be equipped to claim your identity and purpose as you move toward wholeness.

This book is for women at any stage of life. Life experience builds upon itself like a layered map. Rites of passage mark these layers, and they each interact with the others. How a woman came into this world, for example, will inform how she will be during her rites of exile, creation, and death.

While you can jump to any particular season of life, the chapters build on one another. My goal is to teach you the art of marking time and making space for ritual so that each birthday, anniversary, or burial can be done with intention and take its place in your integrated story. So, even if you are a sixty-year-old woman reading this book, it is still beneficial to intentionally mark what you and your body have created. If you are a young woman, it is still essential to understand the rites of death and legacy because these realities accompany us throughout and will be the conclusion of our story.

Ideally, you can read this book from beginning to end, no matter what stage of life you are in, and then return to it over the years as your story unfolds.

Her Rites of Passage

The initial moment our lungs drew in air,
the image in the mirror when we saw our naked form,
the first time we bled or had sex.
The day we walked down the aisle to get married,
or signed the divorce papers,
the last time we bled,
the last time we had sex,
the day we buried our first loss,
the hour we take our last breath,
for these, we have a rite to pass.

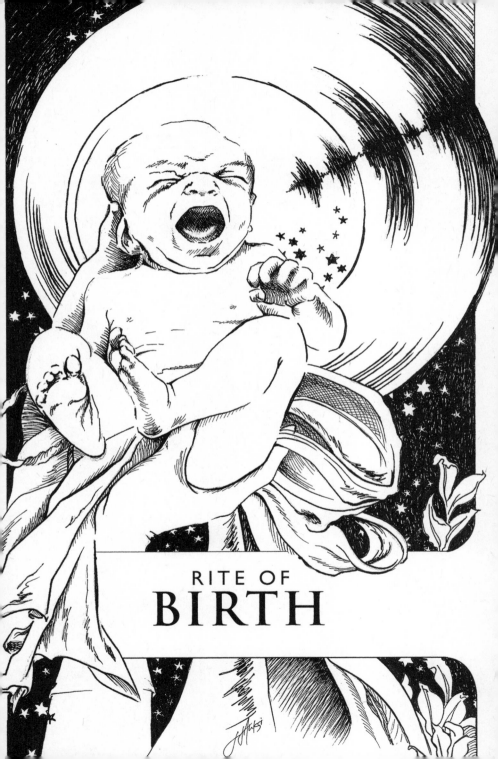

RITE OF
BIRTH

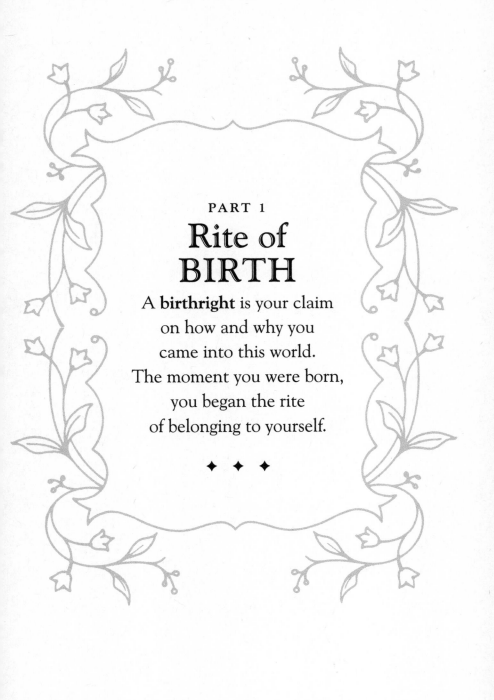

PART 1

Rite of
BIRTH

A **birthright** is your claim
on how and why you
came into this world.
The moment you were born,
you began the rite
of belonging to yourself.

◆ ◆ ◆

BELONGING TO YOURSELF

Belonging is the rite of passage we take over a lifetime,
but it begins at birth.
Every woman belongs first and foremost to herself,
this is her birthright.

"You aren't from here, are you?"

I am standing buck naked in my new gym's coed dry sauna—a sauna I entered from the women's locker room and wrongly believed was an all-women's sauna. I moved from Seattle about a year ago to this small town in the Appalachian Mountains. Three of the 3,386 men in this town looked up, surprised, when I entered the sauna. These men knew I had no clothes under the tiny towel barely covering my body. I froze and stood there, wondering what to do. *How have I found myself accidentally naked in this town's only public dry sauna?* The first statement I said, under my breath, was "We are not in Kansas anymore, Toto." I had never been in this situation. Until now, I had been a strait-laced, somewhat-liberal, law-abiding citizen. I am a Jesus follower who teaches in moderately liberal church institutions about sexual and spiritual health. My mother and grandmother are the most modest women I know, and God knows I have never seen their busts showing in a low-scooped blouse. I was always taught that a woman's body was something to hide. That damning belief prompted me to study women's sexuality for over a decade, and as a result, the signature message of my career has been that God can be known through a woman's body. I stand in front of classrooms and congregations sharing statistics on what Western patriarchy has stolen from female sexual health in multitudinous ways. This kind of teaching was welcome in the Pacific Northwest. But now, standing here barely covered in front of three men in a tiny sauna in the South, I feel my expertise as a sexually healthy Christian woman waver. **Often, the subject we specialize in is what has wounded us most.** But to teach something is different from living it. So here I am, presented in this sauna with an opportunity to be sexually healthy. At this point, it is getting weird standing here. I spot a woman in her sports bra and shorts in the dark upper corner of the sauna. She has earbuds in and hasn't seemed to notice me. All of the men are still looking at me standing there, frozen in place.

Do I turn around or hold my ground?

Have all my years of work on sexual health come to this decision?

Should I stay or should I go? (I mentally sing the Clash version.)

I cinch my towel tighter around my body and sit in the only place available, between two men wearing swimming trunks. The men readjust their positions awkwardly, looking at me as if I should have known it was a coed facility. Technically, there are no private body parts blatantly visible. Yet, I can feel the closeness of the men on either side of me. I sit there with my eyes closed, trying to breathe in the heat and let it warm my body.

My mind raced. *What do these men think? Is there anything wrong with what I am doing right now? Am I tempting these men? Am I being inappropriate? Is the woman behind me mad that I stayed without any clothes? Thank God it wasn't an empty sauna where I had disrobed completely, only to have men walk in on me. Will this ruin my credibility as a Christian female leader?*

BRENÉ BROWN IS RIGHT: THE stories we tell ourselves in these moments are to be explored. I told myself what I had always been taught, that **my naked body is dangerous. My sexual body empowers, exposes, and discredits me all at the same time.** That is the story I told myself, even though I had spent years reclaiming what is most true about my body. I have a good body. A body that has allowed me to play sports, birth babies, bleed, and heal. I have journeyed through my rites of passage as a woman. I have worked to know my birth story, the meaning of my menstrual cycle, and the importance of my sexuality. I have fought the psychological harm of objectification, the worthlessness I have felt when my body is in the presence of men with a pornographic gaze. Yet there I was, claiming the only rite that could not be taken away from me—**the right to belong.** I chose to belong to myself, my body, in this gym, and in my own story, rather than allowing anyone else to take it.

I felt good coming to this conclusion sitting there in the sauna. I would allow the others to have their reactions, but I would choose to hold on to myself—my true self. I slowly opened my eyes when I heard his voice break the silence of the steaming sauna.

"You aren't from here, are you?"

The three-hundred-pound, fully dressed man, including socks and shoes, interrupted the silent, hot space. He had walked in and stood because there was no place to sit. I looked him in the eyes, and my smile broke into a laugh. "No, I am new here." Our conversation was kind, and we talked about everything from cold-plunging benefits on our bodies to the de-policing in Seattle. For most of the conversation, I was unaware of my nakedness; I felt present and clear. Finally, when I reached my heat capacity, I said goodbye and left the sauna. My friend was in the women's locker room, and I told her about my experience. She laughed uncontrollably at my mistake, and I joined in with unabashed enjoyment of the hilarity of it all. I didn't feel embarrassed; I felt proud. Proud that I didn't run. Proud that I held on to myself. I knew this was one of the many moments I had to regain my right to belong to myself, and I would not let anyone take that away.

A few years ago, I prayed for the women at a conference I was leading, and I felt the Lord so firmly say, *Women don't need you, Christy. Lead them to themselves, their true selves. Show women their reflection so they remember who they genuinely are.* I wholeheartedly believe these words. If women genuinely see who they are, all will be well. If you genuinely see who you are, you will be well.

Your body is a road map telling you a story you need to hear. The woman's life story is written on her naked body. "Naked I came into this world, and naked I will leave," as Job says. I will not be ashamed of my nakedness. Blessed be my body and the Creator of all things, for fearfully and wonderfully was this body made.

As you journey through the rites of passage in this book, you will find that some will feel familiar while others will feel foreign. In these chapters, I will hold up a figurative mirror for you, and I want you to exercise the courage to take in your naked reflection as a road map telling you her story.

Stare at her.

Study her.

Remember who she has been, what she survived, and how she will impact this world. If you remember nothing else throughout this journey, remember this. If you can see yourself—truly see her—and hold on to what you see, you will be okay. The grounded, flourishing woman is what the world needs. Finding that woman in yourself begins with learning the story written in your body.

Each birthmark, scar, skin pigmentation, and wrinkle has a story.

Each emotional wound, invisible scar, or Botox-filled line explains what she has endured. The way you engage your body informs how free you are.

THE MOTHER WOUND

"All life has a birthright."

—*Anthony T. Hincks*

Asia has seventy-one million orphans.

Africa has fifty-nine million.

India has over thirty-one million.

Around five million Americans are adopted.

To be orphaned is one of the most devastating ideas I know as a mother. When my firstborn son died, I felt such a deep loss, like an orphaned mother, which made adoption seem like one of the most radical loves I could fathom. What does this mean for the physically orphaned child? Or the adopted child?

"Kip and I are sitting at lunch together and he asks me what 'adoption' means."

My friend Sparrow is sitting in her car weeping. She has just told us that she must find a way to tell her son that he is adopted. Her shoulders shake with heaving breath, and I almost have to remind myself what she is referring to. In my mind, Kipling has never been anything other than her son. I flash back to that night nine years ago when she and her husband called us to their house. They told us there was a baby boy in the hospital, days old and drug dependent, that was given to them. We were a close community, and we realized immediately that they were telling us our entire community was adopting a baby. Kip was in their home within the first two weeks of his life; a few of the women in our church who were breastfeeding pumped milk for Kip in the following months. Sparrow is the only mother I have ever known for him. She sits here almost a decade later and explains that Kip doesn't know what the word orphan means. He knows he had a tummy-mom who birthed him, but he doesn't understand the term orphan. We put our hands on Sparrow's body, and she asks us to give her some time alone. Her motherly love is so fierce, so painstakingly deep. She knows the agony of a mother watching her son lose his naïvete. Letting go is something we cannot fully articulate; it is an internal suffering the mother's love knows.

While everyone must leave their mother at some point, choosing to leave their mother is entirely different for the orphaned child. Physical orphans have an apparent mother wound and a severance from their mother. They will rarely touch their belly button and know to whom it was once attached.

Everyone's very first scar is their belly button. The umbilical cord is knotted, and the scissors are raised to clip the lifeline between mother and child. You may be surprised to hear that I have kept not only the white plastic bobby-pin-looking clamps that were used to depress my children's cut cords, but I have also been known to save the dried flesh that falls off after a few days. It's disgusting, I am fully aware of that, but it is also my child's first wound and, therefore, their first scar. As a mother, I believe I am my children's story keeper until they can remember who they are. Their first scar, the belly button, is a physical marking from their birth story.

Every client in my practice will tell me their birth story at some point. Usually, I give my clients a lifespan timeline exercise to fill out and bring to therapy. Every timeline begins one year before their birth. Why do I do this? Because in my research, I have found it essential to reflect on the emotional climate of the womb's waters. To understand my client's attachment style with their mother, I begin with questions such as: What do you think your parents' relationship was like when they conceived you? Were you a planned life? What were your mother's pregnancies like before you were born? What was postpartum like? It is essential to know your story in total, and thus we start with the stories held in the womb waters.

In her book *The First Woman*, Ugandan author Jennifer Makumbi shares a story with young, native African girls who do not know their birth mothers. Makumbi explains that these girls are adopted and raised by the village of women. She defines the first woman as an independent, "original state of the female who has been all but lost to most women." Once born, women don't generally take on their most authentic form. Our relationship with ourselves is at play here; it impacts much of who we become. Although our relationships with other women also affect our self-growth, our attachment style with our primary caregivers determines our relationship with ourselves and others. Our relationships with ourselves and other women, on the whole, are usually similar to our relationship with our mothers. We look to our mothers to tell us about who the woman we are is. Many of us do not like what we see, and some of us reject it entirely. Becoming the first woman requires us to leave our mothers' attachment style and discover a more primordial way of being connected to ourselves.

What about the emotionally orphaned? The abused? The estranged?

Emotional orphans may have a physical mother who completely abandons them for addictive behaviors or abusive partners. The wound of the emotionally orphaned child is that she has known abandonment at an internal level, which is critical to name. Whether we are mothers who have given up our children for adoption or daughters who have been orphaned, these women have a complex mother wound. Some of us do not like our mothers. Or we do not know our mothers. Some mothers are unsafe or unaware. Some are uninspiring and lost in busyness, anxiety, shame, or being consumed with the self. This makes it difficult for the girl who must find a surrogate to be her initiator. Or worse, some girls have no initiator at all, either at the start or the conclusion of her rites of passage. But these rites of passage allow girls to become women. The female journey through life is a cycle of leaving her birth mother and birthing herself repeatedly, eventually birthing herself through death. Leaving our mothers will expose the damage that our biological mothers and adoptive mothers left us to repair. For that reason, we must identify our attachment styles with our mothers and whatever harm they may have left us with, whether physical, emotional, sexual, or spiritual. As daughters, our attachment style with our mothers may have been dismissive/avoidant, anxious/preoccupied, fearful/disorganized, or secure. In chatting with my attachment specialist, licensed therapist, and guru-friend Eden Hyder on a podcast interview, we explored some words to describe the attachment relationship between mother and daughter. See where you find yourself.

The **dismissive** mother emotionally abandons her child, leaving her to believe there is always something more important than her worth and validation. The daughter of a dismissive mother considers herself too much and over-attends to her own children, abandoning her own emotions.

The **preoccupied** mother turns her gaze away from her child; she will not allow herself to stop doing because this stillness would expose what little of her is there. The mother's anxiety produces an internal voice of inconsistency for the daughter.

The **fearful** mother avoids security and presence because it is too much to love with the incredible potential for loss.

A **disorganized** mother has moments of being both anxious and avoidant. The child has no consistent pattern or structure to know how to have access to the mom. The child can be so scared of some of the mom's reactions that it creates a frozen space for the child. The mom cannot differentiate herself from the child. The child can have intimacy, closeness, and presence if it serves the mom's needs. The other extreme is the mom who will have nothing to do with the child, and she is the opponent or assailant. The child blames herself.

The **secure** mother is courageous in the unknown, offering her presence and confirming to the little girl that she is worth being with no matter what arises. That secure mother can care for her child because she can care for herself. Because she chooses herself first, she can choose the child when their needs arise. The other mothers (fearful, dismissive, preoccupied) are not able, for whatever reason, to care for themselves, and the child's needs are threatening to her.

Identifying your attachment style with your mother or primary female caregiver will allow you to understand your relationship with your internal voice. You speak to yourself in congruence or opposition to how you hear your mother's voice in your mind. Identifying our internal voice is helpful on our journey to belong to ourselves; it will be particularly vital later, when we walk through the rite of exile.

DAY OF BIRTH

"Take a breath. Stop and take a God-breath."

My sister tells her kids to stop and take God-breaths when they feel out of control. God-breaths are the first gift God gave His children: their breath. Our breath has the power to regulate us. Breath is a tangible birthright we receive on the day we are born. A healthy, integrated life requires us to return to our first rite of passage. Breath is crucial to life, and the first breaths are always essential to pay attention to.

To know ourselves better, we must start at the very beginning. When was your first breath? Our bodies hold the story of creation. Conception and birth are important markers in our stories. We are impacted by how we came into this world, but we rarely reflect on it. Understanding their conception and birth can help someone feel more grounded in their story. Our parents or guardians are usually our story keepers until we remember our history. Due to the chaos of childbearing, mothers and fathers may not have had space to document how their children came into this world. Whenever I begin working with a client seeking greater well-being, I start with birth. As I am learning my client's story, she is learning how to tell her story. To remember where she came from, she must first begin by recognizing her story keepers.

Who were your story keepers?

Knowing where we come from becomes a foundational guide to understanding who we are and where we are going. Take the story of Disney's *The Lion King:* the blue-bottomed mandrill, Rafiki, is the rite of passage guide, the initiator for an adolescent Simba to remember where he came from and who he is. In short, the lion's birthright was to be king over Pride Rock and to rule the animals and land his father and grandfathers had ruled before him. He did not know how to lead when he lost sight of who he was. Such is true for all of us who do not know or remember our birthright; we are daughters of God and carry a living legacy in our bodies. We are supposed to be given our birthright on our birthday, just like Simba was presented at his birthright ceremony. We must remember and mark our birth as the day we were invited to take our place in this world.

Our birthing day is a passageway event in life that must be recorded. Conception is the dedication in your life book. Birth is the story of how you were initiated into this life. Consider the place, the hours, and the characters present when you came into this world. We can learn about these details only from those who witnessed our birth, who are our story keepers. Our family members, birth mother, doctor, and other caretakers are our story keepers until we are old enough to remember and tell our own stories.

Days of birth are about recordkeeping and celebration.

Due to cultural shifts, days of birth are less often seen as rites of passage that need a ceremony. While there is much beauty in cultural ceremonies, we know there are also cultures allowing grotesque and barbaric practices among birthing rituals, such as the practice of female circumcision. The female body has historically been targeted to control and alter around beliefs of beauty and sexuality. Women continue to fight for the right to have ownership over their own bodies. When it comes to births, Western medical culture has made some pendulum swings from the cultural practices marginalizing some crucial ceremonial marking traditions that benefit the birth child psychologically. Research shows that restoring birth as a ceremony can promote health equity. In Cherokee culture, the new baby was marked with red seed paint to signify the blood shed during birth and was then washed in the river every day for the first two years of life. In Turkey, mothers of newborns are given a red cinnamon drink to induce lactation, called lohusa serbeti, "postpartum sherbet," which friends sip on when they visit the hospital. After twenty days, the friends return to rub flour on the baby's eyebrows and hairline to give it a long life. In Latin America, *la cuarentena*, "quarantine," is a forty-day observance where the mother abstains from spicy food, sex, physical activities, and housework to focus on the attachment with the baby. The *faja*, "cloth girdle," wraps the mother's vulnerable body: her head, neck, and belly. Japanese culture also protects the mother's recovery after birth, as she spends at least a month at her parents' home being fed osekihan, red-rice-and-red-bean dishes, in celebration. Crying is a sign of health in Japanese culture; the mothers are encouraged to give birth without pain relievers to prepare them for the hardship of motherhood; the Nakizumo cry contest is held because the baby who cries the loudest and most often is believed to grow faster and healthier. In Bali, it is the Hindu tradition that a placenta is treated like the baby's twin and must be cleaned and buried. The baby is considered a divine goddess sent from the heavens, and the baby's feet must not touch the ground for 210 days, but when they do, it signifies their crossing into the earthly realm. Guyana births are celebrated nine days after the baby is born, when the mother takes her first post-birth bath and then burns the placenta to represent the physical separation between mother and baby.

Our grandmothers, midwives, mothers, and doulas are active parts of the birth story worldwide; historically, they are our story keepers. We look to our record keepers to give us the context of our birthright. Mothers will be postpartum forever, unless they do the work of returning back to themselves. A common Asian and South American ritual is called Closing of the Bones. This ceremony assists a woman in returning her spirit back to her body after birthing.

I didn't have a Closing of the Bones ceremony until my forties, years after I was done birthing. Little did I know that I was a mother longing to return to myself. Even more so, I needed to return to myself so that I could engage motherhood. The woman who led me through the ceremony was so kind to explain to me that once we have experienced motherhood—which means infertility, miscarriage, abortion, adoption, or birth—women are always in a state of postpartum. Few of our mothers have been wrapped in a *rebozo* and rocked back into their bodies after giving birth.

CONCEPTION

"That one just made a baby."

I sometimes laugh at my husband when I'm on the way to the bathroom to pee after sex. It's so ridiculous that he thinks he knows when his ejaculation is intense and can impregnate me. At this point in our marriage, he has had a vasectomy but still makes verbal notes when he believes to have offered an intense "baby-making" ejaculation. The point I am trying to convey is that conception matters. It is the prologue to our birth story. Every human has a story worth telling, and the details are essential. Many of us will never know our conception story, but it doesn't mean we shouldn't be good investigators of our own birthright. Here are a few questions we can ask: When, where, and what state of relationship were your parents in when you were conceived or at your birth? How has your story been preserved and told over the years? Has your birth been told in detail, or do you have little knowledge of how you came into this world? Do you come from a family whose photographs line the foyer in beautiful frames, or are there no family photos in your home due to an early childhood divorce? Was your conception a decision made by two parents who wanted a child? Our parents are the most influential people in one's birth story, and how a family tells birth stories offers insight into each child's self-identity. Therefore, we must strive to give the most accurate account of one's foundation. If you intend to consider these stories, your body will tell you. Whether it is by documenting your birth order, studying your mother's culture that influenced her birth and the attachment phase with you, or the shape of your "innie" or "outie" belly button, there are clues that tell us your birth story. C-section scars, blood transfusions, stretch marks, or vaginal tears are bodily scars shaping a story map. Women's bodies are story keepers by nature: they hold stories within themselves.

BIRTHPLACE

"Kids, look, this is where I was born."

Every time I drive back to my hometown, I can feel it. The rhythmic nod of the car tires on the Atchafalaya Bridge could lull me to sleep. My eyes rest on the familiarity of the moss-dressed cypress trees that line Whiskey Bay, and I know I am almost home. Louisiana seems like the kind bastard child of the fifty states. While it ranks as the second poorest, it always welcomes visitors to come inside and eat. I have a love-hate relationship with Louisiana's bipolarity. She offers you the most authentic invitation to belonging, while at the same time, hints of ignorance, good ole boys' clubs, and functional alcoholism reign. When driving there, I often roll down my window and let the balmy, warm air fill the car. My skin is hungry for the humidity and absorbs it like water in a desert. My husband and kids begin complaining as the heat replaces their air-conditioned comfort, and my nostalgia is interrupted by the reminder that they were not born here. Their bodies, not drawn to it like mine, are unfamiliar with this place.

I continue pointing at road signs; my children are unimpressed at best, looking up for a moment from their screens. This is a standard practice my husband and I find ourselves in. We can drive our kids through our hometowns and tell stories that are more alive to us than they will ever be to our children. We wish they could join our bodies in reliving the tastes, smells, sounds, and I want my husband and my kids to somehow transport back with me into my childhood body and feel the humidity bead on my forehead as I run through sugarcane fields in the summer heat. But they have very little desire to listen as we drive through the St. Martinville sugarcane fields and I relive those summers of initiation. For some reason, I keep trying to sell them on my stories, but they rarely have a genuine curiosity for them. In one last, feeble attempt to be known, I blurt out and point to a road sign near the end of a long travel day: LAFAYETTE, LOUISIANA.

The watermelon-rind-green exit sign with a French word across it is of little interest to them. Once we pass these two expressway signs off of I-12 in southeastern Louisiana, we are too close for me to finish listening to my podcast, so I drive the rest of the way thinking in silence. I have never visited the hospital in Lafayette, but I know I was born near this stretch of the road. My mom says that is because our hometown was so small, she delivered all of her babies in the larger neighboring town's hospital. I am her third child, and I don't think she imagined the labor would be as hard as it was. The only image I have from my day of birth is on a film slide, and my small face looks unquestionably disproportionate and swollen from the journey through the birth canal. Born six days after my mother's twenty-eighth birthday, when she was navigating a tense marriage and had two little kids at home, she was nothing less than exhausted. Mema, my grandmother, was there for the birth; she told my mother at six P.M., after hours of pushing, "Sometimes the hardest ones to get here are the biggest blessings."

My grandmother took roses and wrapped them around the hospital bed rails as my momma pushed into labor. I was born at 6:31 P.M. When my mom held me for the first time, she christened me with my birthright, and I would be the daughter who brought hope. Mema recounts my day of birth on my birthdays, telling me how she tucked the roses into the white hospital blanket I was wrapped in, and my two saucerlike, chocolate-almond-colored eyes stared back at her. While my kids don't care much about this story, it feels important to me that my grandmother and mother carry the story in their bones. We must recall the significant players during our day of birth and how much they played in our story.

BIRTHRIGHT DEFINED

Heritage. Inheritance. Right. Belonging. Prerogative. Privilege.

These are the words associated with a birthright. A birthright is a moral or natural right. We are inherently worthy of life as human beings. Knowing one's birthright means naming one's right to receive an inheritance. *Webster's* defines the word birthright as *a right, privilege, or possession to which a person is entitled by birth.* Biblically, Christ eliminated hierarchies of birthrights, laying down his life so that any could receive the inheritance of God's children.

Particularly for women in ancient Israel, the birthright was marked by gender bias. Women did not inherit property or wealth often; they had to contend with Moses himself to change the law and grant them land ownership. Numbers 27 tells how the daughters of Zelophehad believed they were the heirs to their father's belongings after he died. Zelophehad had no sons, raised his daughters under the law, and taught them the way of the Lord. After much deliberation, Moses overruled the law, believing it was the daughters' birthright to receive their father's land. To this day, their persistence has given the women of Israel the ability to inherit land from their ancestors. As women, historically, we must advocate for and demand our birthright in places it has been denied.

Becorah is the Hebrew word for birthright. It is associated with the custom that the firstborn male to open the womb will receive a double portion (Deuteronomy 21:17). Where else do we hear in the Bible about a double portion? Elijah and Elisha. In 2 Kings, Elisha asks for a double portion of Elijah's spirit after he dies, and scripture says that Elisha's ministry saw twice the number of miracles that Elijah did. In the Old Testament, there is still a bargaining system for power and worth, "a double portion of anointing," in which not every birthright is considered equal. But with Christ's death and resurrection, we are freed from this bargaining system, and our inherent value as humankind is affirmed. The greatest act of love overrides the law. The Holy Spirit is sent to dwell amid humanity. The new ruling of love is led by the Spirit, not by the law.

When we break through our mother's womb, we inherit breath. As we referred to it earlier, God-breath is an inheritance of peace that our Creator gave us, the very breath within our lungs, the heart within our chest. We are creations, and we have a birthright. Often we want to overlook this first rite of passage; unless we are born to royalty or into money, we don't think much of our birth as our foundational inheritance. We also rarely remember our rite of birth. There may be a picture or two taken in the hospital room or a specific story about how we logistically came into the world, but that's usually it. Many people don't know the origin of their name or what it means. Yet these moments are markers that help us tell the story of our life and existence.

As humans, when we tell our stories, we must first recognize that we were given a birthright at birth. Each human soul automatically inherits the birthright, but it also means something different to each person. For example, as a child of God, you automatically have a spiritual birthright. In a larger context, every birthright has a psychological significance, such as birth order, gender, and family culture. Our family of origin, or the family we are born into, impacts how our birthright is interpreted. Is my family intact today? Do I come from a divorced home? A sexually or spiritually unsafe home? Metaphorically, did my mother or father hold my birthright ransom from me? Was there a vow made by my parents that kept my birthright at bay from me? For example, if you were a child who favored one parent, did the other withhold from you physically, emotionally, or relationally? Was I given up for adoption at birth or put in the foster care system? What did I physically, emotionally, and spiritually inherit from the parents who adopted me? All of these factors impact our birthright. Our birthright is no better or worse than another's; it is our own and is received differently depending on our birth parents. The details of our birth story are the road map to navigate our rite of passage through birthright.

Birth order, gender, and family of origin are the best psychological context to map your birthright. Although we immediately belong to humanity when we are born, sometimes birth order can put an invisible hierarchical lens on our birth. Are you the oldest, bossy child? Are you the middle and golden child? This might impact how you were treated or how you determined you needed to behave. Gender roles can play a part also. The beautiful daughter? The only boy and the pariah? Family of origin impacts this as well. Are you the one your parents let get away with anything? The one your parents adore? The one your parents hate? Some relationships threaten our sense of birthright, challenging knowing and living in our natural rights. Have your siblings or parents cursed your body, eye color, hair, or singing voice? Has your father named you innocent, provocative, slutty, or his good daughter? Have your brothers teased your weight, breast size, or athletic abilities? Has your mother cursed or celebrated your beauty, talent, and youth?

As you are undoubtedly reading this many years after your birth, it may seem like a strange time to mark your birthright. But there is no right or wrong time to engage in a rite of passage for your birthright. For many women, we have never been taught that it mattered to understand our birthright, let alone claim or reclaim it. Sadly, much of female research is centuries behind; even the medical community reports that research particular to the female body is not implemented in doctors' offices until ten years after it is discovered, due to regulations and rural communities. This is no different for female psychological research. I did not know that the female birthright mattered to the feminine psyche's well-being until I looked at how biblical birthrights were discussed regarding only male children. As I wondered *What about women?* I realized that even today, few are answering this question.

With women in my practice, no matter what season of life they are in, I find it essential always to establish their birthright. Whether I am with a twenty-year-old or a sixty-year-old, it is fundamental to her self-identity to contend with and name her birthright.* Some women already know their birthright. They

---

* As an important sidenote, I will say, if there is acute assault and abuse in a woman's life, birthright might not be the first place to start with care of her self-identity. I would encourage women who are, in a sense, bleeding out in their lives due to sexual abuse, domestic violence, or loss, to first be cared for by a trauma-informed therapist before engaging in birthright rites of passage.

know their lineage, culture, and matriarchal line, and this terminology will feel like old hat. But for most of us, I suspect, discussion of our birthright feels like foreign territory. This birthright rite of passage is for you. As one engages in the rite of passage for their birthright, it involves naming what we have been told by others, whether explicit or implicit, and renaming what is most true about that. At its core, the birthright is about acknowledging that we belong and have value. Those physically, emotionally, or spiritually orphaned spend most of their lives trying to belong. We all want to belong, and truthfully, our birthright is that we inherently get to belong to humanity.

Womanist theologian Alice Walker says, "The most common way people give away their power is by believing they don't have any." It is crucial to reminisce on the story of one's birth, recognizing our birthright was offered to us through the particularities of culture, skin color, and gender. In her book *In Search of Our Mothers' Gardens*, Walker explains that "part of what existence means to me is knowing the difference between what I am now and what I was then." For many clients, untangling ourselves from our mother's and grandmothers' gardens is a lifetime's work. One must name what has been said about her and disentangle the truth from untruths. It would help if you explored old narratives. You must write out your birth stories and answer these questions about the dynamics happening when you were conceived. We are deeply impacted by what our primary caregivers believed we were meant to be to the world and to them. A birthright rite of passage deepens our understanding of who we were and who we are becoming. We must see the birth story as the beginning of the timeline in our lives. It is a marker that helps us know the original intention of our existence.

BIRTHRIGHT VIGNETTE

I began the birthright therapy session by asking Angie this question: "What year were you born?"

"Nineteen-eighty-one."

Angie is looking at me, unimpressed at how my question relates to her sexual and spiritual health, but I continue without hesitation. "Then we start with 1980 on your sexuality timeline." A huge roll of white butcher paper is on the floor next to us in my large, sunlit counseling room. We have a bucketful of markers, and she is kneeling near the edge of the paper with a fluorescent pink marker in her hand. She writes *1980* on the first line and looks up at me curiously, asking, "Now what?"

"Now, tell me whether you believe your parents were in love when they had you."

Angie is again baffled at this exercise and responds like most women working on their conception story in our sessions. "I don't know. How would I know?"

We pause again, and I allow my client to listen to her body's response to my questions. *Were her parents in love when they con-*

ceived her? How would she know? My client can intuit almost 90 percent of the time, even if they are adopted. When they stop and consider what they know about their parents, they often sense where they come from. Sometimes, if a client has had children, I ask them if they remember the sexual act that conceived their child. The question usually brings on a wave of emotion because sexual history is complex. I do not remember the sexual encounters with my husband when my kids were conceived. But if I spend enough time reflecting on the year of pregnancy, the place we lived, and the stage of our marriage, I can get a sense of the sexual season I was in when I conceived.

For instance, I know when my husband and I conceived my second child. I remember it because it was emotional, sad, and in Thailand. It was three months after the death of our stillborn son. Intimacy was laced with our grief and my body's trauma at the idea of trying to conceive another child. I share this to say that many children are conceived in a season of desperation, longing, hope, or passion. Women's reproductive years become a road map for many clients working through their birthright. A woman should always begin with her birth—but this may be informed by thinking about the season of life her parents were in when she was conceived. The stories we are trying to remember happened while in utero, and we have no way of knowing the story of those nine months. So, we must become investigators and put together pieces of the story from what we know now as adults about our parents and what was happening in the story.

I asked my client again, "Do you have any sense if your parents were in love when they conceived you?" Angie looks pensive and bites her lip before emotionlessly stating: "They were not in love. I am the fifth child. My dad was cheating on my mom when she found out she was pregnant with me. She was still breastfeeding my older brother and did not think it was possible to get pregnant . . . she considered aborting me, but my family was Catholic, and my dad told her she could not."

Angie looks down at her empty paper and begins to scribble in hot pink marker, **dad cheating, mom wanting to abort me, mom still in the post-partum with my brother Henri.** I can feel she is starting to wake up her body to the exercise, and I must pace myself not to rush ahead.

"Can you imagine what her pregnancy with you was like? What are the stories told about the day of your birth?"

She does not hesitate for a moment. "My mom called my dad to leave work and get her. She had taken a shower and packed a bag for the hospital. She asked to stop at McDonald's on the way and almost went into labor in the dining area near a plastic life-size statue of Ronald McDonald. When she got to the hospital, she told me it was the hardest birth of all five of her children, and that my huge blue eyes made her feel so much guilt that she had thought of aborting me. . . . she called me her daughter of joy."

Angie is so deep in her story she does not notice she is writing all over the butcher paper and covering most of the 1980 section she has allotted for her year of birth. I do not want to interrupt her, but I want her to begin to reflect on the themes in the story of her birth, so I ask the question, "What does it mean to you to be named *Daughter of Joy* by your mother?"

She stops writing immediately and bristles. "I do not like the title. There is so much pressure. My mom tells me although it was the hardest pregnancy, I was the easiest baby and the most delightful child. She still calls me her Daughter of Joy to this day. She said I never cried much and was always a joy to feed." Though my client's voice is monotone and slightly disgusted, I smile slightly. Angie's countenance has fallen, and I reflect to her, "It sounds like you were demanded to be your mom's surrogate from the beginning of your life." She looks up quickly.

"Her surrogate?" She is nodding in agreement, but her brow is furrowed in question.

"Many children become their parent's surrogate spouse whenever the child is engulfed in an enmeshed relationship. In your case, I think your dad's adultery and your mother's guilt of wanting to abort you made you the perfect child for your mother to become enmeshed with."

My client writes on her paper something I cannot read from my viewpoint. I sit back and let the heaviness in the air settle. When she finishes, her writing is filled with words and phrases:

daughter of joy
  enmeshed and surrogate spouse bound to my mom's
need

Her words all feel correct, so I move on. "When the glory of a human soul is born, each is given a birthright. What is yours?"

"My birthright?" She looks confused again.

I do not stop to answer her. I push on. "I not only want to know your birthright but also, who has silenced it? Like I said earlier, when a human soul is created, glory is inevitable, and usually, evil is somewhere in the birth room also marking your story. What do you think is your birthright, and how has it been targeted?"

Her hand shakes, and I see the words spill across the floor: **I never belonged to myself. I had no voice of my own. I have been cursed. I cannot be myself because I must remain my mother's daughter of joy. If I do not, I will be orphaned.**

She finishes writing, and I bless her courage. She has just told me about her birthright.

RITE OF
INITIATION

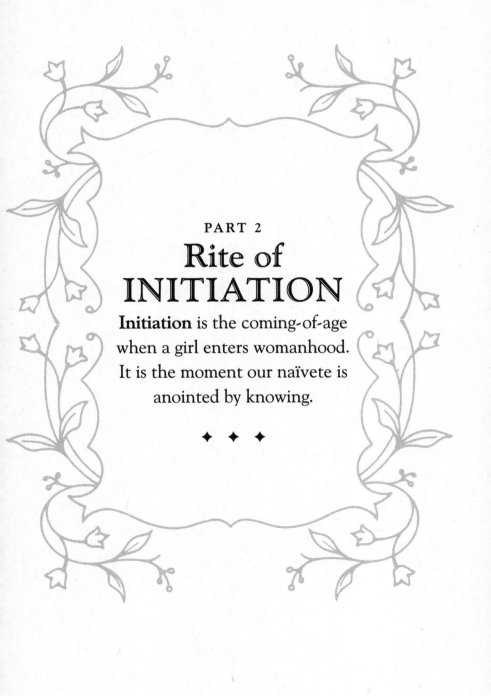

PART 2

Rite of
INITIATION

Initiation is the coming-of-age
when a girl enters womanhood.
It is the moment our naïvete is
anointed by knowing.

◆ ◆ ◆

FROM NAÏVE TO KNOWING

The mask suctions my adolescent face;

my body awkwardly flips over the boat's edge.
The clear blue water remains at bay from burning my eyes,
eyes that see an aquarium awaiting,
as warm salt water buoys my wonder.

Initiation is now.

I will never forget that first moment the water became my safe
place. My parents had officially filed for divorce the fall I
started third grade. Moving to a new city, a new school, and
significantly more modest housing were just a few factors that
tormented my psyche. My siblings and I flew to Belize that
summer to be with my dad. The sea became the only place
large enough to hold my emotions. The Caribbean water was
like a beautiful turquoise field that went indefinitely to the
horizon. My sister and I would sit on the bow of the boat as it

skipped across the delicious seafoam waves and sing at the top of our lungs. The wonder of this new place distracted me from the turmoil of my life back home in our tiny apartment and ruptured family system.

I missed my mother. Like any young girl, the middle child of her family, I longed for a parent who was not devoted to something else more than they were devoted to me. My siblings wrestled with their internal worlds, and I felt the impossible task of taking my mother's role as an emotional anchor. My drive to caretake left me with no haven to find reprieve. I would not find that rest for my divorce-orphaned heart until there was a snorkeling mask suctioned to my face, the awkward flippers on my feet, and I felt that disorientation of leaning backward over the edge of the boat. The warm, crystal water enveloped me like a womb. Every fear and anxiety I had faced over the past seven months felt held. It was as if the ocean covered me in her warm embrace; she knew all the lonely moments I had survived: the tears I shed as I packed up my childhood bedroom and the day I walked into a new classroom. The conversations I tried to have with unfamiliar faces of students while trying to block from my mind the yelling I constantly heard through the paper-thin apartment walls of my new home. My new life. I let my memories tumble out in the safety of the water, away from it all: the water was a respite. The ocean's white-noise heartbeat drowned out all the painful angst. I knew we would be snorkeling for hours, and no one would see the tears that filled my snorkel mask, so I let them flow unabashedly. Snorkeling in the ocean would be a rite of passage into adolescence for me that summer. It was the time when I, just a little girl, awoke to become my own guide, to begin to mother myself.

Coming of age is the foundation of some of our most important stories. It represents the first time one is initiated and is a story worth remembering. Whether it is Mary using the key to unlock the secret garden, Kya raising herself in the marshlands of *Where the Crawdads Sing,* Disney's Mulan leaving home to fight on her father's behalf, or Scout trying to figure out what is right and what is wrong in *To Kill a Mockingbird,* every young heroine is invited into the perils of exploring womanhood on her own. Coming of age is the journey for every young girl, and the ocean's floor was the compass for my rite of passage. Any initiation is usually accompanied by an environment that she finds herself navigating: a relationship, a sketchbook, an instrument, journal pages, or a landscape. You walked through puberty and encountered yourself, discovering if the world would be kind or cruel. Some of us had parents who could attune as good guides during adolescence while others did not.

Of what she never found in her mother,
she found in nature.

I'D RATHER BE A BOY

"Christy, you have to put a shirt on."

My brother yelled across the lake from the raft where he and his friends played king of the mountain. I could tell from the tone of his voice he was embarrassed as I marched my eight-year-old figureless frame down the yard toward the lake. All of the kids in my family had gotten lice two weeks prior, and my mother had all the girls' hair cut short to a boy-style haircut. I was thankful for the excuse to exercise my curiosity about what it would be like to be a boy. I had spent the week walking around in my shorts, exposing my flat chest to the world with defiance for shirtless freedom.

I waded into the dark waters of our lake and swam out to the raft. I climbed on and began pushing the boys off, willing my body to be one of them. My brother was only a year and some change older than me, but I felt his frustration with me when he pushed my body hard off the side of the raft and into the water. I didn't realize that if I wanted to be a boy, I would have to learn they have a pecking order. Although my prepubescent body was not much different in size from my brother's, I felt his testosterone-fueled body fling me again and again off the raft, putting me in my place.

Frustrated and defeated, I swam back to shore and headed into the house. Since that day, I have vowed never to make someone feel less than me. What I also knew instinctively that day was that I was a girl, not a boy. I hated that feeling because I believed boys always got away with more. Being a girl was less than, somehow. In my culture, it was not exciting to become a woman. Girls have always, stereotypically, only looked forward to learning to cook, wearing makeup, and shopping for clothes and products to make them feel more beautiful. Gross. I wanted to puke in my mouth. I vowed never to be an odalisque, bound to makeup, diet, dress, or my figure. I wanted to live free. I was enraptured by stories of young girls longing to be treated equally, such as the Chinese folklore heroine Hua Mulan or Jo March in *Little Women*. I would stand in front of the mirror and recite lines from these stories, particularly the scene when Jo meets Laurie at the dance. He is asking her about her father, and she says, "I can't get over my disappointment in not being a boy, and it's worse than ever now, for I'm dying to go and fight with papa, and I can only stay at home and knit like a poky old woman."

Initiation into womanhood was less than alluring for me. I did not want to be like most of the women I knew. There were no wild, older women whose lot in life excited me to aspire to become like them. I didn't want to grow up and get married and have children. The Representation Project researches girls' interests, and it studies mainstream media and cultural effects of the underrepresentation of powerful and influential American women. Their film *Miss Representation* showed the staggering effects of sexism and media on girls. Kindergarten girls who were asked about their interests mentioned math, science, and becoming president when they grew up. The same girls were asked again in third grade what they were interested in, and they reported being highly concerned about their clothes, body image, and diets. The Representation Project found these statistics (Newsom, 2022):

✦ Women comprise only 4.6 percent of all S&P 500 CEOs.
✦ Women make up 50.8 percent of the United States population.
✦ In the last ten years, rates of depression have doubled in women and girls.
✦ In girls as young as six to eight, one out of every two reports they feel they should be thinner.
✦ One in seven women experiences sexual violence in dating.
✦ Women hold 85 percent of consumer purchasing power.
✦ The United States is thirty-third out of the forty-nine highest-income countries regarding women holding federal elected office.

These statistics illustrate why I didn't want to be a woman when I grew up. Of course, I could see that all the boys around me had the power and privilege that I wanted as an option. But alas, I was a girl.

The rite of initiation is the journey girls take when becoming women. Yet we have lost the desire to be a woman other than a famous, beautiful woman in our culture. This is such a limiting vision of what women were created to be. One of the reasons the idea of initiation into womanhood is not desired is that we have lost the true definition of the woman. My grandmothers were women who ran households, crocheted afghans, and cooked meals. My grandfathers were men who ran banks, developed film in a darkroom, and bought and cultivated islands in the Caribbean. On a superficial level, I had no incentive to pursue femininity when masculinity seemingly had the upper hand in society. Yet when I began to study the core of female traits, I was astounded. Women were made to weave together the most opposing forces: light and dark, spring and winter, hope and despair in such a tight knit that the tapestry the female creates brings forth life. Yet there is a cost every girl encounters on her way to womanhood: her blood.

INITIATION BLOOD

"I never want to do this again." I closed my eyes and pulled the trigger.

It was just before dawn broke when I saw the doe. There were two doe standing in my uncle's meadow that I could easily see through the scope of my gun. I was visiting from college and determined to bring the venison meat back to save some money that semester. My uncle had set me up in his attic window with a cup of coffee, and I was convinced I would never hunt from a deer blind again. Warm and nestled, I spent the early hours sipping coffee and waiting. It felt like I was cheating, sitting up here with a scope that let me quickly shoot the deer of my choice. It was one shot, and I ran down to ask my uncle to help me field dress my game. When I drove down in the truck, he took me through the ritual of honoring the kill I had made. I appreciate this part of hunting, when you thank the animal for giving up its life to nourish yours. My uncle showed me where to cut and explained the different parts of the body. His finger swiped the deer's blood on my cheeks and forehead. I was dizzied by feelings of both pride and disgust. Proud that I could kill my food and provide for myself and disgusted that I had killed an animal at all.

Initiation is about blood. For many females, we may never go out to hunt and kill an animal, but we will know the demand for blood. When blood is shed, we must stop, pause, even for a moment, and attend to it. A scraped knee, a cut finger while prepping a meal, or the blood that tells us we are not or are no longer pregnant—all women must contend with their blood. Initiation into womanhood begins when an adolescent girl begins her period. Unfortunately, Western culture hides the female's period rather than ceremonially recognizing it. So, it isn't surprising I had more profound feelings about my initiation as a hunter when my uncle marked my face with the doe's blood than when I began my period. The doe's blood ran bright red across my forehead. I felt a little sick to my stomach, but I hid the fear, not wanting to be seen as too girly to hunt. Here lay this doe, probably a mother. We learn something about ourselves in initiations. I realized that day that I don't enjoy killing; if I must, I'd rather hunt fish in the ocean than mammals on land. What I learned in becoming a hunter: I don't like the blood and I would rather bleed than kill.

CAMO OR FINS?

His voice is hushed when he answers the phone. *"I'm in Me-meem's duck blind."*

My brother has never been known for getting up early. I don't call him before noon. Yet my brother is like most men from the small southern Louisiana town where I grew up; he loves to hunt. As we whisper our conversation during the call, I can almost see his breath in the cold air as he speaks. I imagine his body crouched, almost lying down, as he silently waits as the dawn breaks through the trees, illuminating the dense forest.

Growing up in Cajun culture, they teach you two things: how to hunt and how to cook. Sadly, I wasn't very interested in either. I inherited a hand-me-down camouflage onesie at eight years old to wear on hunting weekends. This was long before onesies were popular and considered cool to wear. Long days were spent on our ATV, riding through the mud, building shelters, cooking food over a fire, decapitating snakes, and tying them onto the grill for skinning later. I didn't love what I felt like killing an animal, and even more than that, I could not handle skinning and cleaning them. There was always an underlying fear in the pit of my stomach when I set out for a day in the woods.

I was not born a huntress of the land.

But I began to explore what it meant to be a huntress. The huntress is the woman who is always looking for opportunities to explore the unknown, to use and show her emotional abilities to find purpose and exemplify the meaning of life. I came from a culture where I wanted to find my own connection with hunting. It happened when I began to study that globally women have hunted in the water.

I LEARNED THAT WOMEN LIVING near the ocean were called sea huntresses. For example, the Haenyeo women in the Pacific Islands harvest through various seasons of production and restoration. It wouldn't be until I explored the ocean floor with spearfishing that I enjoyed hunting. The freedom of the snorkel allowed me to breathe with ease as my eyes scanned the underworld. The hum of God's womb in my ears as I searched for conch, lobster, and fish. I felt the excitement of hunting pump through my blood. My dad put a speargun in my hand, and I felt at home hunting.

Men could hunt the land, but this woman wanted to hunt the sea.

Sadly, my mother never taught me how to be a huntress. All of her energy was used to survive PTSD from an abusive marriage. My dad took to heart that he had three girls who didn't love holding a gun, so he taught us to hunt the sea. The ocean became a place where my father and I could connect. What men must have felt when they woke up early to go hunting, I felt as I slipped on my snorkel and slid into the crystal blue water. A world awaited me, a living kingdom to be explored. I identified myself as a spearfisher and prided myself on having enough of a "man's sport" to keep up conversations about hunting with men.

I felt at home as a huntress of the sea until I got pregnant.

At that moment, my entire being went into "building a life" mode, and I could not bear to have anything to do with death. Pregnant and sitting in a bay window, I stared at a doe eating my aunt's beloved garden. They kept the gun nearby for these very occasions, but I could not move. I would not kill something while I was actively creating life. There are seasons in hunting to give animals time to replenish. There are seasons in farming when the land needs to replenish nutrients. There are seasons to the year so the world can continue flourishing. My female body was teaching me that there are seasons that I must also honor.

I began to find and understand the huntress within myself.

The huntress in me began to mature into someone who knows the balance of life and death. When it comes to creating life, it takes everything in me. My body naturally knows how to create, realizing the all-encompassing cycle of life and death. My reproductive years consisted of six pregnancies: one stillbirth, three live births, and two miscarriages. Life was so expensive to me, and any type of death was not an option during these seasons.

Through seasons of adolescing, reproduction, and menopause, I realize I am still learning about my inner huntress. In the days, months, and years that pass, I have to explore the new spaces that come with growth and aging. There are many different seasons for humans: waiting, risking, sleeping, and learning are just a few. Each of us has an inner huntress within. Mine surpassed spearfishing, and even though that is my favorite sport, the huntress in me awakens when I am in a new land that must be learned and explored. The huntress emerges, and excitement begins to bubble under the surface.

DANA AND GOLIATH

Her dark, black marble eyes met mine fiercely. She was strikingly beautiful to me at that moment; I had never noticed how much she looked like a cartoon princess. Yet it was four A.M., and she was only five years old, and I was so tired of caring for her after hours of vomiting and diarrhea. An odd tingling fills my body in the midnight hours when my kids wake me up when they're feeling sick. Once I moved past my years of bated-breath anxiety, a wild, mother-bear, superhero excitement started to take over in these middle-of-the-night moments. Sometime after I began to believe that God was just as much Mother as He was Father, I felt a calling and a purpose to act like Mother God in the midnight hours of my children's need. While I can protect my children from a few things in this world, I always have the power to comfort them. The mother's body is where kids can find refuge from their fears and comfort for their hurts.

We were staying in a large rental house, and my sweet girl had found her way down the unfamiliar staircase to my bedroom. Her stomach was hurting, and we quickly went to the bathroom. I had been in a deep sleep and threw myself into the needs at hand. Cool rag, check. Ponytail back her hair, check. Rub her back as we sit with our faces closer to a toilet bowl than anyone ever wants. Following a stomachache, our tradition of care is always a middle-of-the-night bath. I drew the water and let her stomach rest in the warmth. She was settled now that she was emptied, and I watched her play with a marble she found at the bottom of the tub. She asked me why glass marbles didn't break when she threw them. I watched her for a few minutes, picking up the smooth marble and aiming it at her target. I was tired, and the initial energy of Mother God's care started to wane after aiding and cleaning. I wiped her face. She asked me to tell her a story; her piercing black eyes shone like dark stones. The scene of her aiming the marbles and her dark eyes reminded me of perfect river stones for a slingshot, making me think of the story of David and Goliath.

I settled in on the cold tile of the bathroom floor and began to tell her the story of a little shepherd boy named David. I watched her eyes glaze over a bit at a story of another boy hero, and she interrupted me with her request. "Mom, didn't little girls do anything for God in the Bible?" She was so honest with her disappointment that I pushed past my sacrilegious shame and dared myself to tell her the story differently. In the privacy of the bathroom walls, I risked dreaming about a litany of Bible stories with girls as the main characters. It was a stretch for me to think it was a little girl who had taken on a giant bully that had offended her God. Still, my daughter's eyes were longing as she watched me, and I told her, "This is the story of a little shepherd girl named Dana who was the youngest of eight sisters. She spent her days with her dog, Danger, and she whittled a slingshot as the sheep grazed . . ."

Immediately, with those words, her five-year-old body, which looked fragile from the upset stomach, showed wonder and interest. She watched me steadily with her black-stone eyes reminding me of the five stones David picked and took with him. My daughter was now fully enraptured by this idea. She listened to this Bible story with more excitement than she ever had a Bible story, and I realized that it mattered that she could picture herself in heroine stories. She sat up straight and tall when I got to the scene of Goliath bullying her family and friends, and she outright snarled when I yelled Goliath's mean words at God.

The exhilaration I felt showing my daughter the care of Mother God turned to trepidation. I wanted to know myself as heroic and brave on behalf of love winning. Finally, something came over me in that small, white-tiled bathroom in the middle of the night. I puffed up my chest and, in a strong voice, confronted the Goliath in the story. "'I am Dana, Daughter of Yeshua, Daughter of the Great Creator, and I am here to silence you. For no one talks about my Creator this way.' And she put the stone in her sling and silenced Goliath once and for all."

The small space got loudly quiet. My daughter and I stared at each other, both enthralled with such a tale. We sat silently for a minute before I heard her whisper, "That's the kind of girl I want to be, Momma." I smiled and handed her a toothbrush, turning on the shower. I wasn't sure what I thought about my story; my seminary professors' voices were rolling around in my head. But, if I was honest, I liked the story I had just created. I wanted to be the character in my story: a little girl who fiercely intends to defend her Creator and go out and battle the bullies and the giants who curse beloved humans.

"But how did Dana get to be that kind of a girl?" Her question came between spitting as she brushed her teeth.

Somehow the need to sleep didn't cross my daughter's mind. So we filled up the tub with fresh warm water. In total commitment to following some biblical history, I told her that in those times, when God anointed someone, His power was upon them. But, of course, my daughter did not understand the idea of anointing, and so back into the tale we went.

I told her that, weeks before Dana confronted Goliath, she did very little but tended to her family's sheep. Dana was dozing off in the warm afternoon sun when her dog, Danger, started barking. Dana saw a great woman with long hair and a noble headwrap walking up the hill. She introduced herself as Abijah, the great prophet Samuel's wife, and that she had come to anoint one of the daughters of Jesse and Nitzevet. With full excitement, Dana accompanied the great prophetess Abijah to her home. When they were close, Dana ran ahead, yelling that one of her sisters would be chosen today as queen!

My daughter and I were enraptured with how this story continued to allure us both, and I knelt next to the bathtub's edge to prepare for the anointing ceremony. Thankful for a fifty-thousand-dollar seminary degree, I knew the scene of David's anointment in great detail. I explained that all eight sisters were brought out into the yard and lined up. The neighbors gathered to see which of the daughters would be chosen. Dana was confident it would be one of her two oldest sisters, but the prophetess passed them by, making Dana wonder if it would be one of her prettier sisters, Zeruiah or Abigail. Still, the prophetess walked past. Dana could now smell the scented olive oil that dripped over the sides of the horn whenever Abijah shifted too quickly. The whole family had heard stories that the prophetess had mourned the end of King Saul's reign and was reluctant to follow God's command to anoint someone new, especially a queen. *How could it be that one of Dana's sisters would be the new queen?* It was all too much to take in, so much so that Dana did not realize the prophetess was standing in front of her. Danger barked, and Dana quieted her dog. Then looking up, she saw the horn spout pour thick, fragrant oil onto her forehead.

My daughter watched me dip my cupped hands into the bathwater and pour it onto her head. She smiled, closing her eyes as the water dripped down her cheeks. We were both pleased with how this story turned out. I whispered, "*This* is anointing, sweet girl."

Anointing is the christening for the rite of initiation. *The ceremony of initiation is the first time we learn something for ourselves.* Yet the rite of initiation can happen over and over again. It cannot be contained.

It is the first blood we feel pouring down our legs in menstruation.

It is the saliva of another that we taste when we are first kissed.

It is the first time arousal lubricates our vagina in pleasure.

It is the man's semen we discharge after the first time we have sex.

It is the first time we feel amniotic fluid wash our babies out of our womb.

It is the milk that drips from our nipples to breastfeed.

These are all passages we journey through when experiencing initiation. The initiated female is invited to experience herself moving from naïvete to knowing; other times she is demanded.

Sometimes they happen against our will. The moment we try something we didn't think possible and see that it can become our own.

Do you remember your rites of initiation? Do you remember who initiated you?

What aromas, touch, or tastes do you remember? Initiations are held in our body memory. The body remembers the smell of the flowers outside our parents' front door or the taste of the oranges we picked in our grandmother's backyard. Body memory is stored after an impactful moment, and then can resurface when that same smell or touch happens years later. Sometimes the body memories remind us of an event we wish we could forget.

DIVORCE

An Emotional Initiation

The relationship between mother and daughter is complex. It is often a wonder our mothers can stay sane through our childhood; we are grateful when they don't leave us alone in the scary world, but when we grow up, we see more clearly what it took for our mothers to keep a grasp on sanity. Listening to our bodies is usually costly, especially for women, for the female body is loud and complex. We have unseen needs that our brains and uteruses ask of us, and we often try to put off what our bodies ask for so that we can meet the needs of those we love. Time and again, a woman negotiates between her body's needs and the needs of the other. It may be with her husband, partner, children, grandchildren, and others close to her— maybe exercise, food, self-care, work, school, and duties. There is always an internal balancing act that women embody differently from men.

Often, to her disdain, I write about my mother in my books. The problem is, I don't have another mother to write about. There is a well-known story about my mother and her white cat, Snowball, who was a gift from my father when my parents were newly married. My mother loved this kitten dearly. It was as if the white, flawless animal represented the early unmarred love between my parents. Tragically, one day, Snowball was run over. My father was desperate to see that tender love in his wife's eyes again, so he bought her another white, flawless little kitten. My dad walked into the house with his gift the week after losing Snowball. My mother looked up and saw the new, little white feline with a bow around it, and her body tensed up immediately. She recounts the whispering words in her mind: *I will never love you, kitten, as much as I loved Snowball.*

This story might tell you something not only about my mother's heart, but also the heart of anyone who gives themselves over to the hope of unreserved love. That day, my mother vowed never to love another cat as much as the one she first fell in love with. The same vow held with her husband years later when she lost him to his failings; she never loved another man as she had once loved her first. When my father's infidelity killed my parents' marriage, my mother's heart knew initiation. She now knew divorce. Mothers teach their children what they believe. Even if a word is never spoken aloud, a child knows what their parents feel about marriage. My mother taught me that when we love uninhibitedly, we get marked so severely that we can never love that deeply again. In my own story of love, I went into an intimate relationship having already lost my first love, my father. Physically, I look just like my dad, with the same chocolate-brown eyes, the same dark hair, and a replica of his jawline. My father was my hero until he wasn't. I recounted the day he left me, and the vow I made to never love another man that deeply.

Grad School Tragedy Assignment: "The Day My Parents Divorced" (Fall 1987)

I skidded my tires along the cement garage floor and threw my bike against the brick wall, only to complete my competition by racing to the back door in victory. I had barely beaten my older brother, and the rare win showed upon the sweat on my upper lip. Dad had called us in for a family meeting, but my recent victory kept me from noticing the house's mood. Instead, I plopped my seven-year-old frame on the couch next to my sisters and watched my brother come in with the frustration of defeat as he grabbed the chair furthest from me.

My dad was talking in a quiet and solemn tone, and I settled deep into the couch and gazed at the sunset reflecting on our shiny mahogany coffee table. A collection of fingerprints was scattered across the glass plate in the center. The curtains behind were partially closed, and I recall my annoyance that the mood would not tolerate my getting up and opening them wide to flood the room with light.

". . . you all know that your mom and I fight all the time."

What is he talking about? I quickly turned my attention to his last sentence. *Fight a lot? That is not true. I have never heard them fight.* I scanned the room to see my siblings' faces; all eyes were on Dad.

I turned to follow their gaze and remember seeing his small lips frame the words ". . . so I am going to be living at the camp for a little while."

As if these words were the gunshot to signal the start of a race, an eruption of voices intermingled at once. My older sister was screaming that it was unfair for him to leave and demanding he stay. My brother was in tears, grabbing my father's legs precisely like we all would do when he returned home from work, making him play monster and carry us around on his feet.

My heart beat louder as I realized he was on his feet. Darkness swam through my chest and stomach as I watched my daddy walk toward the door. The chaos in the room stung the back of my eyes as I looked to find my mother seated quietly near the door.

His oversized silhouette filled the foyer as he opened the door to leave, and as everyone exited the house, I was left alone for a moment.

All I could hear was the sound of the ocean in my ears.

The way it sounds when you put a conch shell to your ear, a mixture of waves intertwined with a soft noise-maker. My father used to bring them home from diving trips and let each of us take turns holding the shells up to our ears, searching to memorize the sound of the sea.

I heard his car start, and I ran to the door. Looking out, there was a scene from a horrific plane wreck, and I watched my family's bloodied and mangled bodies scatter across our yard.

My brother was on his bike chasing my father's car down the road as he screamed at the top of his lungs, begging my dad not to leave him. My older sister was halfway down our driveway crying, her body lay across the asphalt, and my mother was attempting to carry my baby sister down the road toward the other two kids.

His car turned right and traced the path we would always take toward our family camp.

I have never felt so empty in all my young life, as if I had watched my father choose to shoot a bullet right into his chest as he stood in front of his four children, with four copies of his own huge brown eyes looking up at him in disbelief.

I remember very little else of that day, I think we all went to our rooms, and I watched my sister fall asleep to the uneven rhythm of my brother's kicking the top bunk bed in his room. After a few hours passed, it was dark; I crept into the hall and put my ear carefully against my parents' bedroom door. I could hear the faint sound of my mother crying, so I moved away from her room, sat against the hallway wall, and cried too.

My daddy was gone, and now we were all alone. I realized I did not have any time to say goodbye to him. I wish I could have at least said goodbye.

I love my father, but because of his choices, I will never be able to love him the way my childlike heart longed to. When my father walked out on our family, my heart broke, and I, like my mother, vowed never to love anything as much as I naïvely and unwaveringly had loved him. Yet, a knowing happens with suffering and death that accosts us into maturity. I sometimes wish I could have the freedom of innocence in my relationships. Being orphaned, divorce, death, loss, and betrayal mark the heart in a way that cannot be unmarked. Yet, when I bravely allow another to run their fingers across the emotional scars of my life, I feel love and connection anew.

I have been an intimacy junkie for decades. Most of my high school and college years were filled with traveling. I fell in love with adventure to protect myself from falling in love with a human. Years later, I realized I didn't like the rite of initiation—it held the shame of the inexperienced. Once I have lived through all my "first times," I enjoy fantasizing about the past. For example, present day, I will always choose a coming-of-age romantic comedy if given the option. It is my guilty pleasure as a grown woman. It is a safe place for me to fantasize about a time when young love could save me from the broken heart I received from my father. In coming-of-age scenarios, I feel the hopeful wave of potential that the boy might redeem what my father broke. But this belief meant it would never be safe to marry. So as I moved on, I traded my adventures overseas for counseling experiences. I got a degree in therapy to become an expert at awkward, intense, and powerful conversations with others. I spent work weekends navigating clients' most intimate stories. I lived for the high of seeing, connecting, and being present with others. I also loved having another leader or facilitator see into me and unlock the secret places inside my story. I became infatuated with this world of therapy that was so intentional and meaningful, but infatuation is short-lived, and love is long-suffering. I became addicted to the hits of quick intimacy and found a distaste for the long-suffering of realistic boredom. This continued to fuel my vow to never truly need contentment, or commit to another.

Mothers teach daughters how to find their contentment. Daughters learn when they look at their mothers to make a note of what holds their mother's gaze. In my family, the women work their asses off chasing success. I come from a line of women who learned how to make their own money because men weren't trustworthy. I was taught self-sufficiency under the guise of independence, but my true motivation was fear of abandonment or betrayal. As a result, I became more bound to my anxiety, although I thought I was helping myself become an independent woman. The lesson is one that every mother teaches unconsciously; her way of being in a relationship with her life partner exposes her children to a road map of relationships. Our parents' love story is a rite of initiation for every child who grows up and becomes a lover.

INITIATION BY THE SEA

I come from the warm,
Caribbean waters of the middle ocean,
nestled between massive bodies of oceanic seas.

At the quiet foothills of the coral reef,
you can find me submerged in Mother Earth's womb.
I am at peace there,
surrounded by the strongest hum of white noise,
the sea life swimming as methodically as the nurse shark hovers
    over the ocean floor.

Here, when I can retreat
to the boat's hammering power
crossing the surface
and the roaring wind deafening the world's chaos,

I feel at the doorstep of home.
The water's color shifts to deep,

cobalt blue and I rise to grab the anchor.
Here I take my only tools, my mask, and my fins;
and I am set free when I dive in,
free to be nothing more than alive and alone with myself.

When I am away from my motherland, I still look for her.
My soul is always searching for remnants of her touch,
her love.
Near the Canadian shores,
I look through the cold rain to be met.
My heart resonates with the waves that splash against
   Northwestern cliffs,
the sound is like a faint memory of my mother's hum when I was
   rocked in her arms.
Water, you are my home.
Sun, you have become my initiator.

The kids are doing rest time, my husband and toddler are both asleep, and there is a thirty-minute window for me to make this happen. I grab my fanny pack—yes, my fanny pack—car keys, wallet, and hotel key. The click of the door closing is like a gun firing; my time starts now. I race to the elevator, and it isn't until I hit the ground floor that I realize I have only my bathing suit on. *Oh well,* I rationalize, *we are in a beach town, and people go to the store in their swimsuits all the time here.* I walk in and make a beeline for the sunscreens. There it is—Panama Jack tanning coconut oil. Yes, I do fear skin cancer, and I feel tons of shame that I often forget to put sunscreen on my kids, but sometimes, when you have very little time to tan, you get desperate.

I wince at the $14 beach-shop markup, but I hastily buy it anyway and head toward the shore. Now I am practically sprinting to the beach chair outside our hotel. I lather the oil over my stretch marks and jiggly thighs, lie down, and let the sun darken my skin. I realize as soon as I close my eyes that I am still wearing my Tevas. I sit up and unstrap my sandals. I probably have about seventeen minutes left before my littlest wakes up. So, I lie there and let the sun burn my skin. I am lucky to have God-given olive skin, which, when tan, covers a multitude of sins. I am grateful for the blazing sun, which holds my eyes shut. Though I cannot see my body, I know the scars, marks, and stretched places it bears. In the quiet warmth, I begin to bless this forty-year-old body that has birthed four children. I bless the stretch marks, my children's artwork, giving evidence of their lives. I look up to ensure no one is around, and then I open my knees to let the sun tan my inner thighs. Lord knows I have had healthy thighs my whole life. My momma refers to my hips as birthing hips, but truthfully, I don't know that they helped my labor. I let the light shine on these places that haven't seen the sun in years. Although the first three-fourths of my life was spent in the humid, blazing southern sun, for the last decade, I have been hibernating in the Pacific Northwest. Vacationing on the East Coast reminds my vitamin-D-deficient body how much it has missed the warmth. Even more than that, my body remembers this ocean.

The Atlantic Ocean, in some ways, has marked significant moments of initiation for me. I learned how to surf these waves at dawn the summer after my high school graduation. I remember paddling out in the cold, dark water with the threat of sharks always tingling in the back of my mind, along with the foam of the waves on my skin. The Atlantic Ocean and I have a history with my lovers. In these salty East Coast waters, I have swum, made out, and made love. The Atlantic has held my budding body and erotic awakenings of initiation.

The last time I was here in Myrtle Beach was the summer I

turned eighteen. Just after graduating from high school as salutatorian in my class of thirty-two students, I was clueless about where I would go to college and what I might study as a profession. Most of us can say of our eighteen-year-old selves "I was young and naïve," but growing up in a very conservative Christian home and school, I was not only young and naïve, but I was also sheltered and inexperienced, mainly when it came to sexuality and relationships. Heading to the East Coast for a summer to participate in a Christian leadership training program was the first time I left home on my own, and my parents hoped I would get a little life experience under my belt before going to college. Along with a few thousand other college kids, I was given the opportunity to work at grocery stores and businesses for a summer internship. To my embarrassment, the Kroger seafood department scooped me up immediately when they heard I was from Louisiana and had experience cutting and filleting fish. I probably wasn't very alluring as I expertly deboned salmon while wearing a chain mail sleeve; the boy I was crushing on opted to ask my roommate out on one of our routine rides home from work. He was a Midwest farm boy with some New Testament name like John or Paul, who was also a part of our leadership summer program and worked in the produce department at my Kroger store. I was sure he was flirting with me every time he walked through the black double doors and smiled at me in the seafood department. I should have known when he offered me and my roommate rides home every day that he was after her and not me, but I thought he had me ride in the back of his truck only because I smelled so badly of raw fish. I was oblivious to the clues of relational interest. Yet, it was one of those summers one never forgets: independence, living with other college students, and sheer newness. I fell in love with every guy there at one point or another. I saw goodness and excitement every-where I looked, whether it was a New York accent or a blond-haired, blue-eyed co-worker in the seafood department. I was there for the ocean, Jesus, and a boyfriend. I spent every day in the Bible and the ocean that summer, and eventually, against all smelly odds, I got a boyfriend. David was my first summer ro-mance, and we ended up dating off and on for the next six years.

The nostalgia of that fateful summer made twenty-two years seem like a lifetime ago. Lying on the sun-bleached pool chair, hoarding my Panama Jack coconut oil, and my stolen thirty minutes away from kids, I can barely remember that summer of first love. I try to picture myself back then, so naïve. I look at my phone and see I have eight minutes before returning to our hotel room. Yet eight minutes for a mother of three kids is an eternity to daydream into fantasy. I sit up and laugh out loud as I realize this is the same city, the same beach, the same ocean where I spent that summer twenty-two long years ago.

As I let the sounds of the ocean waves wash over me, I hear that eighteen-year-old girl telling me how she remembered that summer. In actuality, I was a clumsy, pious girl, but in my mem-ory, my felt experience was that her tan, toned body and her heart desperately fell for a boy and his motorcycle. David and I hadn't been hanging out for long when he offered to take me on a ride. All of me, and I mean all, came alive when I rode on the back of his bike. My arms around his chest and my breasts against his back were my initiations into sexuality. I was never graceful or sexy, and in an attempt to get off of his bike at the gas station, I accidentally leaned against the blistering metal muffler and singed a baseball-size burn on my calf. I remember explaining to him that I didn't need to go to urgent care. I told him I had gotten burned plenty of times at the beach, and my dad had shown me salt water would create the fastest balm. My dad taught me the ocean cures everything—every boredom, every heartache, and every pain, including burns. So I pleaded with my new crush to drive me a few blocks to this very ocean in this little town and leave me there. David was reluctant but he listened to my wild pleading and drove me to the ocean. I didn't want him to see me cry as I forced myself to tend to my throbbing leg, so I waited until he walked back to his motorcycle. He was hesitant to leave me, but I was insistent.

I remember the walk to the water, how badly it hurt stepping deeper into the ocean, the salt water submerging my singed-raw skin, my flesh screaming. I remember not turning back to see whether David had driven away. I remember the tears that came until I was so deep that I could only taste the salt from the sea. This was one of many times that mother ocean would soothe, wash, and drown the grief that comes with initiation.

My phone's alarm wakes me from this daydream. My time is up. I rise reluctantly from the beach chair, grab my fanny pack and the coconut oil, and return to the hotel. I look down at my left calf as I stand waiting for the elevator; the twenty-two-year-old scar is barely visible from that burn many years ago. The salt water was an effective balm and continues to be.

My love stories are not merely of men, but of the elements of the sea. My body has always gravitated to the ocean; she parented me. Whether in the early years of swimming in the Pacific, snorkeling in the Caribbean, surfing the Atlantic, or cleansing myself through miscarriages in the Northwest Puget Sound. I know the water; she has been at times my father, my mother, my God incarnate, my enemy, my partner, my friend, and my lover. While Mother Earth, whether mountain or ocean, parents us, our mothers often bear witness to us in our years of initiation. We hide the lipstick or perfume we stole from their makeup counter. Sometimes we ask them for advice or to borrow their shoes. We run into their arms after our hearts are broken, or we lock the bathroom door and hide our tears in the hot shower steam. But after the rite of initiation is completed, the daughter begins to leave her mother.

LEAVING OUR MOTHER'S HOUSE

Initiation is an action, an act of ritual, in which someone passes into a new life stage. But diving further into the historical context for initiation, we learn that this is a natural part of existence. On the African plains, the mother lioness must train her cubs to be self-surviving within the first years of the cubs' lives. The initiation ceremony often resembles a mother forcing her reluctant cub to take down a wildebeest from behind. Cubs are unwilling to learn how to kill for their food, yet if they never know, they will be dependent and probably die. Survival in nature demands initiation, and our mothers are our teachers. If our mothers do not teach us, someone must. Often in therapy, female clients can quickly name the harm from their fathers. Historically, a woman's covering was passed from their father's headship to their husband's, which is why married women must often untangle themselves from the constant male dominance that has been a part of their story. Marion Woodman's book *Leaving My Father's House* is a researched passageway of a woman's journey from the impact of her father's world. While we can see the tangled subconscious web that women must unravel to get their fathers out of their minds, it is even more difficult with our mothers.

Psychologically, the relationship between the mother and her child is complex and even more tricky for daughters. For some of us, if we look closely at our birth stories, we can see that the moment we were born, we became something for our mothers. Daughters can be their mother's delight or disgust, something for their mother to consume or alienate. I would love to live in a world where everyone is loved perfectly by their mothers, but that isn't the case. Sometimes our mothers cannot lead us, and they refuse to do the work to understand the typical dilemmas of womanhood, such as sexuality, beauty, eating disorders, femininity, alcohol, employment, financial power, and interdependence in relationships. Mothers teach daughters how to interact in this world. Girls must be allowed to explore who they can be as women. Much like the lioness with her cubs, a mother prepares her daughter for initiation into womanhood. Or she doesn't. And if she doesn't, someone must.

INITIATION DEFINED

Initiation is the threshold of experience.

Initiation walks a girl to womanhood through physical rituals that put us in an elite club: bra shopping, DivaCup insertion, wedding dress shopping, getting our cherry popped, signing divorce papers, skinny-dipping in public, and orgasming sweetwater.

Initiation into a rite of womanhood is ceremonial.

BAT MITZVAH, QUINCEAÑERA, AND MENSTRUATION ceremonies are a few common rites of passage that initiate us into coming of age. Yet there are many less culturally informed rites of passage—things like hunting, cooking, sewing, and building. In addition, initiation into womanhood includes naturally feminine experiences in adulthood, such as romantic relationships, infertility, pregnancy, marriage, and divorce. Each of us may experience initiation in numerous ways throughout our lives.

Initiation rites of womanhood are both psychological and

physical. Psychological initiation is about wonder and maturation, whereas physical initiation is about capability and growth.
Physical rites of passage into adulthood are commonly about
one's body adolescing, or growing into puberty. Physical initiation into womanhood might look like budding breasts and buying a bra, bleeding, using tampons or pads, engaging calories and
body weight, or the act of pregnancy and miscarriage or birth. In
biological terms, we see that a girl is initiated into womanhood
when her body sheds her uterine lining repeatedly in preparation for future phases of reproduction and menopause. The initiation rite of femininity is the birthplace of creation and will
lead us back to our intuitive selves.

The female's body offers an exquisite picture of all that is
powerful and powerless in the same space. Lifespan psychology
posits that if we follow the story of the woman's uterus, we learn
three repeating cycles over the lifetime: life-death-life. Coming
of age for a girl is the initiation into the cyclical rhythms of a
woman's body. The initiation rite of womanhood marks when
the doors of enlightenment open upon you—such as when you
go to the bathroom and find blood in your underwear or feel
pleasure surge through your clitoris. Initiation is the feeling you
have when you walk down the aisle at your wedding or feel another enter you for the first time. These moments can happen in
the complexity of navigating your parents' divorce or your divorce or a passionate kiss after passionless love. Initiation is
coming into a new experience that you have not ever had.

Psychological initiation happens to women throughout their
lives; some examples include betrayal from a trusted partner
and burying a beloved relationship. Another one, less named in
Christian circles, is a woman's first sexual encounter with someone without fully being present in her own body. The rite of
initiation happens all the time as we walk through life; it is the

rite of passage from naïvete to experience. When our psyche completes a new passage it has never experienced before, we mature. The woman going to therapy for the first time shows up in her maturation differently than a woman who has been in therapy for five years. These are rites of initiation that lead us deeper into our knowing self, constructing our intuitive self. **Initiation is the moment you move from unknowing to knowing.** It is an anointing of sorts.

INITIATION VIGNETTES

"I gave him a blow job. I had never done anything like that before, but somehow I felt so aroused, and I went for it. At first it felt so powerful, and within seconds I felt like a whore."

In my therapy sessions with Megan, we focused on narratives of sensuality in her life. She had told me the story of her first shame-filled sexual experience. She was in graduate school, about to graduate with her master's in business. She explained that she felt insecure that she and her boyfriend weren't having sex until marriage, and they had decided oral sex was a good level of intimacy.

"Now, we have been married for four years and I have little desire to have sex at all. The idea of giving him a blow job is repulsive. When we told our pastor, he told me I just needed to give him more of the kind of sex he wants."

When Megan said the words aloud in my office, she looked away, refusing to hold eye contact. While I wanted to address the pastor's idiotic instruction, I knew that attacking patriarchal doctrine was futile at this moment, so I focused on my client. I wished she had looked away with shyness, but I knew it was shame. *Shame. Again.* I have seen it innumerable times in my office: shame suffocating healthy expressions of love. She continued without looking up, "I was so attracted to him back then. We were so physical, and I was turned on by it. Now I am tired and bored when it comes to sex." Megan was crying now, tears slipping down her cheeks, dropping periodically onto the rug as she continued. "I think I was only aroused because it was forbidden. My husband thinks my sexuality is broken."

Sadly, this is common to hear from women who grew up in conservative environments. We all remember when our bodies woke up to sexuality. The moment his hand brushed against ours, catching eyes from across the room, a first dance, first kiss, or when our own body felt a tingling sensation that kept all other thoughts away. Often that quick moment of breathless-ness can be hijacked by shame. Many of us have known the sting of shame through a father's admonishment, a teacher's disapproving look, a mother's cutting words, or a chaperone's glare.

Here's the thing: Shame poisons sexual health. Women's sexuality has only recently begun to be seen as a health matter; for generations, sexuality was viewed primarily as a means of procreation. When women grow up in a hyper- or hypo-sexual environment, their view of sensuality is often skewed. Many of my clients who have been sexually abused realize their hatred of the penis is connected to their true hatred of the vaginal canal because it can house the penis. Another way to consider this is the woman who seeks a safe type of arousal through fictitious or fantasized scenarios: the girl who reads romance novels but is afraid to have an orgasm. For a woman who cannot safely enjoy sexual development, she creates for herself a different infra-structure of arousal: celibacy, abstinence, friendship rather than romance, or asexuality. These contexts produce less shame for her and thus a safer place to desire.

The rite of initiation may need to be a reclamation of what has been taken from you or was never given. Often our stories of crossing from places of unknowing to knowing are marked with shame. Pleasure is such a vulnerable emotion, and sexuality is fueled by pleasure. Guilt and shame often creep in when we risk an area where we have little experience. Briefly, I want to delineate between guilt and shame. Guilt is the belief that there is something inherently wrong with the action I am participating in, while shame is the belief that there is something wrong with me personally.

A rite of initiation is a vulnerable crossing over when one actively learns a new way of doing something. This vulnerable space must be parented well, and sometimes we are the only ones who can tell ourselves that it was courageous to experience something new. The feelings Megan felt when her pastor spoke those words of judgment, "Christian women pleasure their husbands," were connected to her physiological experience of shame. The foundation of her sexual development was poisoned, and she came to feel the effects when she couldn't experience pleasure. Reclamation aims to initiate the body into a place of new knowledge, parenting oneself into the initiation of wholeness and maturation. So, what rite of initiation is beckoning you? Is it the reclamation of your body, your inner huntress, your holy bleeding, or knowing sexuality?

MAY YOU RECLAIM WHAT has been lost, shamed, and broken—may you be initiated into a fuller and knowing version of yourself.

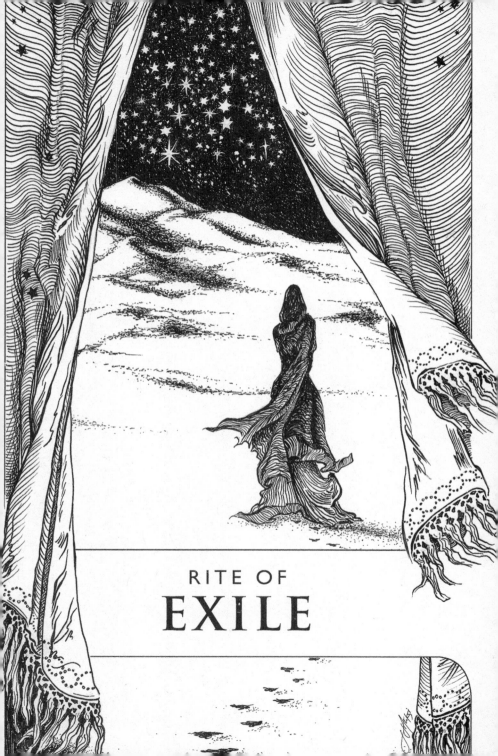

RITE OF
EXILE

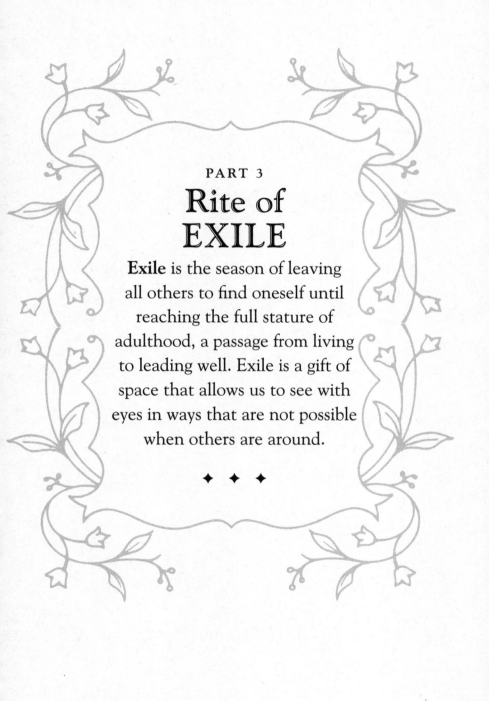

PART 3

Rite of EXILE

Exile is the season of leaving all others to find oneself until reaching the full stature of adulthood, a passage from living to leading well. Exile is a gift of space that allows us to see with eyes in ways that are not possible when others are around.

◆　◆　◆

WE'VE ALL HAD TO SAY GOODBYE

We've all known that moment when we must say goodbye. The farewells from high school to college. The last time we kissed a lover. The night you stayed in his arms until dawn, savoring the final minutes until you drove away with tears streaming down your cheeks. Exile often comes when we end a relationship. I can sum up some of the most heartbreaking moments in names. Tom Vidrine. Chrissy Brooke. Mema and Awpa. Jared Ellingson. Sarah Trahan. David Grotheim. The Breakfast Club. Tim Wilson. Autumn Grace. Andrew James. Brave Bauman. My Seattle sisterhood. After my parents' divorce, I lost having my father in my everyday life. When best friends moved away or boyfriends didn't stay, those goodbyes brought on seasons of exile. If you have ever sold a home that held significant meaning or left a community you loved dearly, you have known the ache of loneliness. The dog you drive to the vet to put down after it has accompanied you faithfully through many years of life. The songs you cry to in your car alone because something has been taken away. Exile doesn't happen once in your life.

Seasons of exile usually begin after saying goodbye to a person, pet, or place where we experienced love.

Maybe it isn't one of those; maybe it is an anniversary, a date that marked you.

December 8.

June 6.

Or an address you called home.

8725 Evanston Ave N.

8914 Aurora Ave N.

A season in your life that was magical:

The fall of 2009.

The summer of 1998.

Exile began the last day of summer camp in 1998, when everyone said goodbye and headed back to their homes. I was starting college in Louisiana on a full scholarship but wanted desperately to go out of state. The drive home from a summer of new friends who were going to other colleges was excruciating. I was the loner. My cousin and friends I had roomed with all summer were going to Texas A&M. My parents, alumni of LSU, were adamant I wasn't going to A&M and pay out-of-state tuition. There are hundreds of moments like this in everyone's life—when we feel the taste of loneliness and we make a decision that changes the course of our lives. When we are young, we don't like exile; most of us can't bear to say the goodbye, so we hold on. We marry the person we are dating because we can't fathom a world with anyone else. For some, we go to the college our parents went to instead of the one our heart dreams of exploring. Learning to be at peace with seasons of exile can give us the greatest clarity . . . yet loneliness is hard.

Exile is visceral when you enter it: The last word is spoken between lovers who are ending their relationship. The moment your chest tightens with pain from loss and panic from the immediate void. When we say goodbye for good, the isolation of life without them sets in. We find ourselves in exile.

My dad was the first man to break my heart. He walked out on our family and stopped fathering me. He no longer tucked me into bed at night; no more stories read to me when I was scared. He was gone without my consent, and I learned that exile from our family of origin leaves a lasting scar, the growing belief that there is no trusted relationship but within oneself.

Exile begins when things stop: No more handwritten letters are in your locker. He sends the last text, and you delete his number from your phone. No one offers to pick up takeout on their way home to you. No one crawls into bed next to you at night. Exile is just you. Only you. For me, it has been moments when even God can't seem to be found.

LEAVING THE RED TENT

To appreciate exile, we must first know that we belong.

The red tent is a historical metaphor that comes from Anita Diamant's book by that same name, and I think it is useful to describe the symbolic place where we learn what it means to belong and where rites of passage happen. The tent is outside the tribe encampment, in the wilderness. It's where women come to be born, bleed, birth, doula, and die. But there is one rite of passage that one cannot do in the red tent: exile. Exile happens to women not only in relationships; it happens in one's career or life calling.

All of my life and all of my career, I have gravitated to groups of women. Finding a career as a people-pleasing Enneagram type two—the so-called Helper—was sometimes challenging. Before deciding to attend a junior college without declaring a major, I visited twelve colleges, received scholarship offers at four, and attended one for two weeks. But I needed more clarity on my calling. My parents were frustrated.

I had thrown away multiple scholarships in order to attend a college where my friends were. I had a history of letting my heart lead, but I usually liked where it led me. My privilege allowed me to coast through college with an undeclared major and to take interesting classes, hoping one of them would woo my heart into a profession. I worked three jobs and traveled internationally on every semester break. I had a wandering soul that led me to earn degrees that would allow me to work with people. Other than those unfocused undergrad years, my career started to carve a path when I went to grad school for psychology, and by the time my doctorate came around, I was focused on women's health. My professional life overall has been such a fun journey. After many letters behind my name and hundreds of thousands of dollars in school debt, I could work doing what I loved, and with people I admired working with at that.

It wasn't until a few decades into my career that I realized I loved to research and teach about sisterhood because I never wanted to leave the sisterhood. My passion for women's connection and friendship allowed me to hide from the work I needed to do in my marriage and in relationships with male friends. I was enjoying a season of working with incredible women when my co-workers called me out on my hiding. I will never forget my colleague and friend Tracy Johnson's face as she looked me in the eyes and said, "Christy, you cannot stay in the red tent forever; you too must go through exile. I am holding the tent flap open until you leave."

Although Tracy was speaking metaphorically, and she promised to be there when I returned, I was terrified. I hate being alone. Alone. Every rite of passage allows for us to have someone accompany us—to hand us a pad underneath the bathroom stall when we are bleeding, to hold our eyes as we count seconds between contractions, to bathe us after our body has been abused, or to sing over us as we take our last breath. The rite of exile is the only unforgiving one. We must be alone, and we must explore the inner voice we hear in the loneliness.

PREPARING FOR EXILE

"I laid my baby far across the desert from me so I could not hear his cries. I told God I was okay if I died here in the desert, but do not make me watch my son die." Her voice cracks, and I look up from scolding my child. "I can't handle that."

She stands before our church, teaching about Hagar's prayer in the desert.

Cathy Loerzel has been in our church for a few years; she is a brilliant, prolific speaker, and I rarely hear her cry onstage. She had never been a part of our community's inner circle, and I realized she was teaching about exile in the desert while living in relational exile herself. There is an arrogance, I am ashamed to say, that has come with my church community. As a founding member of our community, when we buried my son Brave, I felt an entitlement to the closeness I had in my church. Because I had started the church with these friendships, I felt entitled to them somehow. I felt the conviction at that moment, and I was Sarah, the one who had cast others out and held tightly to my delusion of God-answered prayers. At that moment, I willed myself to listen to Cathy's account of exile in the desert, thanking God that I had already lived through exile in grief and would never have to go again. I looked around the church and felt gratitude and possessiveness for my friendships in that room. Little did I know that one doesn't graduate from exile; it can happen again and again.

I think there is a particular rite of passage that everyone fears, and the rite of exile is mine. Alone in the desert, listening to your son die in front of you. This is my worst nightmare. Hagar had no choice. A man in a man's world raped her body; her offspring was an outcast because of a woman's jealousy. Hagar never wanted to be in the position she was in but she contended with God, cried out to Him in the desert to save her son Ishmael. And in the story, God speaks to Abraham and to Hagar, but he doesn't speak to Sarah. My pride of close friendships would not save me from exile. It wouldn't be very many months after Cathy's sermon that the pandemic changed the landscape of our community. Our pastors transitioned out, families moved away, and my sisterhood unraveled. My exile began when my husband and I decided to move across the country leaving everything we had built together—our home, our jobs, our community, and the land where our firstborn was buried. I remember trying to prepare for the ominous coming of removal. Frantically, I looked through journals from the season I pilgrimaged after my son died. I tried to gather any wisdom to take to the desert this time. When my husband and I lost our son, we tattooed his name on our wrists. Countless times I found myself getting a glimpse of the permanent ink and being thankful that I had some remnant of him still on my body. So, I did whatever a good, progressive, Christ-following woman does. I headed to an all-women-run tattoo parlor and marked my body. The birds I had inked into my skin were intended to accompany me whenever the desert would come. Yet in my naïvete, I didn't realize that in the rite of exile no one comes for you. Although my intentions were noble, Cathy's tears had been preaching something I didn't want to hear about—when you are in the desert, your friends can't come for you. Hagar's prayers proved that there is no one in exile with you but God. And the tattoos I had intended to comfort myself with were much more like Ishmael's wailing cries reminding me of what had to die to complete my rite of passage through exile. In the desert, all there is to keep us alive is our conversations with God.

DESERT EXILE

Throughout the seasons of my life, and especially in seminary, my faith has been tested by fire. I've had spiritual seasons where I ran to people and community and refused to let go, rather than to God to hide with Him in the mountain's cleft. My darkest night of the soul was my son's death. I did not believe God could understand what I was grieving, and I cursed His maleness because I wanted Him to understand what it felt like to be a woman and a mother who had buried her child. God had to show up as a Mother, not just a Father, and God did. God reminded me that I am made in His image *as a mother*. My career took on a whole new depth; women's well-being became something I realized God was passionate about. I wrote an entire book on knowing God through a woman's body. In that process, I immersed myself in studying the idea of the red tent. I learned that God had a story for women.

I loved the red tent and the women I came to know and the things I helped to birth within the red tent. But as things become our sole lovers, we are always asked to give them up. I idolized the sisterhood and the career I had made, and I never wanted to leave. So, as I mentioned earlier, when my colleague Tracy told me I had to leave and go to the desert, tears filled my eyes immediately. I knew she was right. And although I cognitively understood the need to leave, all I could feel was the pain of exile.

There had been seasons in life when I constructed a false exile in the hope that my isolation would teach me what God wanted me to learn from true exile. When grieving my son's death, I studied the discipline of the meditative monks and the ways of desert mothers. But exile can only be learned in exile.

It was on that cross-country trip. We packed up our family of five and said goodbye to Seattle after fifteen years of creating a community. We sold our house. The first house I had ever owned, a home we fully renovated from basement to attic, in the neighborhood of church friends with whom we built a community of care. Cabinets I painted in the night hours while my babies slept, and a doorframe on which I etched their height measurements. The walls of that house held my shouts of positive pregnancy tests and sexual pleasure. Those same walls held my angry cursing in marital fights and hot tears of grief when blood came though it shouldn't have. But I didn't just sell the physical home, I sold the land that surrounded that home, land that I worked season after season. The land I lay on for countless hours watching my children play in the backyard—with lawn chairs and picnic blankets that hosted friends and playdates with endless conversations. Every inch of our property held priceless memories. I am a child of divorce. So when we sold our home, my body reverted to that third-grade girl who lost her childhood home, her parents, her siblings, her stability, neighboring grandparents, aunts, uncles, and cousins.

As well-trained therapists who created an intentional family system, our family of five said goodbye to our home and Seattle community. We drove out of our neighborhood, past the grocer I went to weekly, the streets I knew by heart, and headed east. With each aching mile that passed, my fear and grief built. The mountain ranges began to look different, and I no longer recognized the land. We were physically heading to the desert, and my body knew it was a rite of passage for me, one of bitter loneliness.

We were outside Moab, driving through the most exquisite snow-covered mountain range, when I heard one of my kids ask for something, and I moved to the back seat of our van to help them. My daughter noted that my eyes were bloodshot from crying. There is no hiding crammed in a van on a cross-country road trip. My children knew I was distraught from the last few nights in close-quarter hotel rooms I had spent weeping in the bathroom, grieving and resisting traveling further from our life in Seattle. Because there was no space, I would try to contain my tears on the drive and then hide in the shower weeping at night. But even the shower water could not muffle my cries. My husband did not know what to do, because he was excited about the move, but he did his best to empathize with my pain; he sat silently on the bathroom floor as I wept.

Yet, even in my grief, we were still moving, getting up each morning and physically driving across the country to this new place. My internal narrative was frantic, and I could not regulate the young girl inside of me who had lost it all once upon a time. I watched the endless miles pass through the back seat of the van window, and I felt gutted, scared, and resistant to transition. I panic in exile. I reached for the handle of the sliding van door, thinking that maybe if I just jumped out of the car, I could end this severe pain and fear that were suffocating my inner thoughts. I shook myself out of it and instead pushed down the lock on the sliding door and moved back to the front passenger seat. My husband was driving while listening to a podcast and barely noticed my arrival. Embarrassed from days and nights of unrelenting tears, I hesitated to say anything. With every silent second that passed, I knew I had to tell him. I mumbled the words out in shame: "I almost opened the sliding door and jumped out." He listened, but he kept driving. That is what exile feels like; no one understands what you are experiencing. But exile cannot be done with another, not even your partner. I knew my husband loved me, so I wondered why he wouldn't turn the van around if he knew how sad I felt. Why wouldn't he rescue me? This is a common question for our Creator during one's rite of exile. Why don't you rescue me, God?

RAGE COMES IN EXILE

"Fifty bucks if you jump in with him."

My husband's voice was hesitant but coaxing, and my children and nephew were excitedly chattering. Although we were parked in front of this lake of cold mountain water I swam in regularly, I was not excited about jumping into the frigid forty-degrees-Fahrenheit water in my church clothes. However, my nephew was visiting for the holidays, and his fourteen-year-old's spirit of adventure was palpable from the back seat. He was willing to jump in for a mere twenty dollars. The extra fun money tempted me, and the memory I knew I would make with my nephew sealed the deal, so I agreed. We ran off the dock, fully clothed, into the icy water that day. My kids watched from a warm car and my husband filmed it. I explained to everyone the entire way home that jumping into a cold lake for a fun memory is very different from swimming in cold water.

Initially, I was highly averse to swimming in cold water. I remember the first time I said yes to cold-water swimming. My Seattle neighbor stood at our fence and asked me if I had a wool cap, and my forehead scrunched up in confusion. She explained that she was a cold-water swimmer and would like me to join. As one always up for an adventure, I agreed against my will. For twelve years in the Pacific Northwest, I had avoided the glacial rivers and lakes, my body strictly protesting my love for snorkeling in warm waters. I didn't sleep that night in anxiety over the cold I anticipated the next day. After school drop-off, I met her at the lake, and she carefully explained Wim Hof's techniques as we entered up to our waists. There we stood, exhaling deeply until our bodies acclimated to the cold. I was surprised that I began to feel okay, but I wasn't going to admit it because I knew the next step was to glide in, and I was terrified.

The largest exhale, maybe even a little cry, escaped my lips as I slid my upper body into the forty-one-degree water. Michelle looked at me kindly as we started crossing the lake. When I finally dried off and jumped into the safety of my car, I cursed and swore to myself I would never cold-water swim again, until I found myself thinking about the experience for the rest of the week. I felt energized throughout the day, proud of myself, and slept like a rock that night. Although I didn't try it again for weeks, I went again a few times, my interest and courage growing each time.

Here I was, a few years later, having left the Pacific Northwest and moved to new frigid waters. During that season of starting over, I found myself drawn to the cold mountain waters. This time, I would use the cold to exhale my anger. I would stand waist-deep in the dark, murky waters and picture all the things that enraged me, all the grief one feels over losses incurred when I left our community, and I plunged into the water, exhaling a sound that expressed my inner feelings. For the first time, I longed for the spiking pain of the cold against my skin. My body wanted to rage, and this became my sanctuary of release. Like a good Catholic who goes to confession, I expressed my inner anger in hopes of receiving absolution. Cold water became a place of therapy for me. I knew there were physical benefits, such as muscle repair, immunity support, better sleep, and pain relief, but it held more psychological care. This act of cathartic release gave me such comfort. This practice became a friend to me.

EXILE DEFINED

Exile is the rite of passage that unearths the depth of a woman's perseverance. Exile awakens her drive to continue no matter what, and the adversity becomes her strength. A place where she sees her reflection in the mirror, and she barely recognizes the woman who stares back at her because the female rarely sees her face as it endures exile. Surviving exile doesn't take your breath away the way that creating does. Instead, it makes you strong enough to face your coming death.

In exile, the female confronts the internal mother. Her voice forms a narrative inside of us, determining what a good mother is and a good child is. Exile is a conversation with our inner voices. Whether the legacy your mother has given you is one of a collapsed, venomous, or fearless heroine, the internal mother is loud during exile. The inner mother has four familiar voices that align with our attachment style: dismissive, anxious, secure, or fearful.

✦ The **dismissive** mother voice is about *worthlessness*. It says, "I don't matter. I am insignificant."

- ✦ The **anxious** mother voice is about *powerlessness*. It says, "I have no autonomy, no control; therefore, I must keep moving, and do more."
- ✦ The **secure** mother voice is about *safety*. It says, "Tomorrow will come. I am okay no matter what happens. Tomorrow will come."
- ✦ The **disorganized/fearful** mother's voice *taunts and is scared*. It says, "Trust no one, nothing is reliable. There is no safe place."

In the desert, we first confront the voice of our mothers, the internal critic of how things should be. We also remember the mother figures and our physical mothers, aunties, tias, grandmothers, and sisters. Their mothering can be heard deep down within us. In solitude, we often hear the biological mother's voice the loudest. Maternal comfort does not equip us to survive severe loneliness. We learn resilience in the wild, not nursing at the breast. In exile, we need a voice that understands the wilderness. If we can confront and silence the voice of the mother, we can listen to another, the voice of the wild woman. The wild woman's voice is intuitive and often heard behind our rib cage or cradled within our pelvic floor.

As we wander through exile, we hear all the voices and visit with them until we hear our own internal voice wrangling them into submission. Exile is the gift of isolation. When we stay in exile long enough we begin to hear our real voice. All the mean and accusing voices we first heard settle and we hear a more honorable voice, our own. Exile is the rebirth of abandonment, giving each woman a choice to choose herself. Being alone long enough to give birth and embrace your true voice as a gift.

ADVENT AS EXILE

"Who are Elizabeth and Mary?" I yell aloud to no one and pose like I've pressed my *Jeopardy!* buzzer.

Sometimes I pretend that in heaven, God and I will play *Jeopardy!* together. Obviously, God would be Alex Trebek, and in my daydream, I am always competing against C. S. Lewis and Delores Williams. Then God would read the prompt "Biblical Women Who Endured Exile." Mary and Elizabeth every time. Williams would probably beat me, but Lewis wouldn't have a chance. The first few chapters of Matthew and Luke tell us Elizabeth and Mary knew exile.

Let's start with Advent. Advent is the liturgical marking of exile. It is a time on the Gregorian calendar of winter solstice, when night comes early and light is more scarce. A time on the church calendar when we wait in the darkness. The main events of Advent are Elizabeth's and Mary's pregnancies. Here's how I tell the story:

Over two thousand years ago, Nazareth was a barren and sparse town surrounded by mountains and hard to get to—the town was no more than four hundred people. Nazarenes drew their water from a well, which was where women gathered to share news from neighboring towns. Thirteen-year-old Mary would have probably been collecting water for her family when she heard the news that her eighty-eight-year-old cousin, Elizabeth, was pregnant.

She walked home, water jug above her head, pondering this news. *How would she tell her mother? Elizabeth, who was in the line of the high priest Aaron, but was never able to bear children for the first eighty-eight years of life, now pregnant? Could this mean she was the one who had been prophesied about in the synagogue, the one who would carry the Messiah? At her age? How?* Her husband, Zechariah, was ninety-nine years old. Mary laughed a little thinking about them having sex. But the woman at the well had said that Zechariah was no longer able to speak. He had been serving at the temple and supposedly he was confronted by an angel.

When Mary reached home she told her mother the news. Astonished, Anne sent word to her great-niece, offering to come and midwife, but heard that Elizabeth was in seclusion, unwilling to take visitors, and that Zechariah was mute. All we know for sure is that Elizabeth went into seclusion for five months. Her own mental exile.

I think about what those first ninety days must have been like, before she felt any kicking, before her body showed signs of pregnancy. Did she have morning sickness and wonder if maybe she really was pregnant? Exile is when there is no one who can answer your questions, no one who can walk through the rite of passage your story is in but you.

It wasn't long until an angel visited the thirteen-year-old Virgin Mary and told her the same news of a pregnancy. Maybe Mary was more prepared because Elizabeth's news of pregnancy had recently come? Those days, in Nazareth, most homes were small, one-room houses. If an angel came to Mary, her mother most likely knew. I imagine Anne, with a history of three husbands, realizing that her own daughter, unmarried, also needed to hide in seclusion. She probably sent another message to Elizabeth explaining what had happened and asking if Mary could visit and be her midwife. Elizabeth sent word back, inviting an inexperienced thirteen-year-old, now pregnant, from a backwater Roman province, to travel alone eighty-one miles to Elizabeth's home. The journey was long, and Mary embarked on her rite of exile, probably experiencing morning sickness as she rode with a travelers' caravan.

Mary arrives tired and uncertain, and she is greeted by her older cousin, whom she barely knows: Elizabeth, who greets Mary with a six-month belly carrying John the Baptist. Elizabeth's husband, Zechariah, welcomes her with no words. I wish I could have stood there and watched that moment transpire. Two women bewildered by their Creator must have felt some relief to see each other. Disbelief and exile now met with miraculous proof and sisterhood.

Mary remains here for months and midwifes for her second cousin, John the Baptist's, birth, and perhaps as she midwifed, she put her hand to her expanding abdomen with a new perspective. The only imagery I can imagine of this moment is Jacopo Tintoretto's painting *The Birth of Saint John the Baptist*. Nestled in the Chiesa di San Zaccaria in Venice, Italy, Elizabeth has just birthed John, and Mary is depicted offering her left breast to feed him.

Now, I am a wild theologian who bore children and breastfed. When my youngest son was in the NICU, I pumped so much milk I was able to donate it to Northwest Mothers Milk Bank. This scene of John the Baptist's birth is such a wonderland of ideas. Mary has midwifed a birth and Zechariah is now able to speak. The whole scene feels heavy with internal realities that God has a wild story in mind.

Mary leaves and travels home to Nazareth with only enough time to tell her mother about Elizabeth's birth and pack her bags for another journey to Bethlehem. Joseph has gotten her a donkey because she is well into her third trimester and cannot walk the entire way. When Mary reaches Bethlehem she is ready to give birth. In the manger, she will have no one to midwife her baby. Elizabeth is back home in Judah, her mother in Nazareth, and she has only farm animals and her husband to help with the birth. She probably coaches Joseph on what to do as she breaks her body open, allowing the blood and water to flow. This is the only way to birth anything. A woman must open her body, and bleed.

Mary, at thirteen, has just birthed exile. Elizabeth, at eighty-eight, has birthed exile. There is no age for the rite of exile. It comes at all ages. Little did these women know that the births of their exile were only preparing them for more exile, the death of their sons.

BIRTHING EXILE

Marriage can be an exile.
   Singleness can be exile.
   Pregnancy can be an exile.
   Divorce can be exile.
   Motherhood can be an exile.
   Widowhood can be an exile.

I IMAGINE MANY WOMEN HAVE, in desperation, wondered why God wouldn't rescue them from the situation they were going through. Particularly pregnancy. I was never that woman who dreamed about getting married and having kids. Don't get me wrong; I love my husband and children. But I was not the kind of woman who fantasized about a family. Instead, I spent an entire decade traveling the world. In my twenties, in addition to grad school, I visited twenty-two countries. There was a summer teaching English in Wuhan and flamenco dancing in Sevilla; I ran with the bulls in Costa Rica, studied Spanish in

Monteverde, climbed volcanos, and soaked in the hot springs of Arenal. I backpacked through Slovenia, visited art museums in Croatia, and explored the ancient aqueducts in Greece. Climbed the steps of the Eiffel Tower, biked the Drielandenpunt in Vaals, and motorcycled through the countryside of Venice. Met my sponsor child in Chiang Rai, rode elephants in the Golden Triangle, and became very comfortable with slingshots and monkeys in Lopburi. If that wasn't enough, I hiked twenty-one waterfalls in the Dominican, smoked cigars on Playa Flamingo, and danced with the Maasai tribes in the Nairobi deserts. Worked in orphanages in Lithuania, kite-surfed in Canada, and hitchhiked in Zimbabwe.

It was as if I couldn't get enough, the world was my lover, and I was its most faithful mistress. For some women, travel is not their passion. What I knew was that travel was a safer hobby than dating. The woman within me loved the earth, a gift from her Creator for her to know Him through His creation. The church frowned on my wildness; every Christian school, church, or college implied that my calling was to be a "good" woman, an Eve or a Mary, who would be a mother and bear children. But, coming from a family of divorce, I felt there was nothing safe about becoming a wife who had children. In my mind, it was a trap. I vowed never to be in the situation I saw my mother in: cheated on and poor. I earned my master's and doctorate with a passionate commitment to making my own money if I ever needed to leave my husband. At the commencement of my thirties, having traveled the world, I was in a dilemma. Although I loved the adventurer in me, I wanted a partner, someone to see the world with me. Being a wife and mother still sounded binding to me, but I was drawn to the challenge of such a mortal path. Could I be both free and partnered? An adventurer with children? I am sure the desire to be both lived deep within me.

I remember finishing the 588th step of the old Karavolades stairs in Santorini and getting to the top, turning to my sister, and telling her that I was ready to get married.

My wedding night was terrible. I cried putting on my going-away dress, bawled driving to the hotel, and told my new husband I didn't know why, but I couldn't stop crying.

Trauma. Growing up in a conservative church with an unfaithful sex addict for a father will wreck any woman. All the strength I had gained learning different languages to live all over the world and earning degrees to keep me from financial dependency were not enough. The exile I felt in the marriage vows was irreconcilable during those first years. It wasn't my husband; he was pretty great. But I was a hot mess. Anxious about sex and fearful my husband wouldn't stay sober from his previous porn addiction. It was a wreck. And then we decided to have kids. After all, I was already in my thirties and close to having what is considered a geriatric pregnancy. I can't say that I loved being pregnant. Pregnancy became an exile for me. My firstborn was stillborn, my subsequent two babies came healthy and alive, two miscarriages, and then my baby boy sent me to the finish line of my thirties.

The story goes that when my last child was born, they rushed him to the NICU and my husband followed. As they sewed me up, my midwife and friend Alyssa asked me if I was crying for joy that he was alive. I looked straight at her and said, "My tears are because I am so thankful I never have to do this again." I thanked God with every fiber of my being that I was done being pregnant. My son and I were boarded in the hospital for four weeks, and as soon as I could drive, I checked out and took my husband to get his vasectomy. I was so thrilled to be done having children, but little did I know that exile was not through with me yet. Now it was time for motherhood.

I understand that this is not all women's experience, and in fact that this might not be many women's experiences. Only each individual woman can say if singleness, marriage, pregnancy, or motherhood was an experience of exile. Here's the thing: I *love* my husband and I *love* my children, and I *love* the seasons of motherhood. But it doesn't make up the complete woman I am. While I think the seasons of exile in these rites of passage are entirely worth it, others may not. It seems essential for me to name that there were long stretches of exile in marriage, pregnancy, and motherhood. I am indebted to God for the gifts of a partner and children I was given. The seasons of exile in relationship with them were brutal at times, and I was able to see the fullness of my womanhood. Speaking for myself, I needed to be independent, a free adventurer, while I also wanted to be a partner and mother. Not every woman is offered these options. For some women, singleness is exile, while for others, it is freedom. For others, motherhood is exile, while it is fulfillment in another. Marriage is a dream come true for many, and marriage is the ball and chain for another. Many women I know found such freedom in divorcing an abusive husband, while divorce for some is an expensive and lonely exile. Widowhood has been for many an anguishing exile when they least expected, which is often how death steals from the living. Exile is the rite of passage. It comes for women differently and in divergent seasons. No matter how exile comes, we are always confident of its closing remarks. Exile always ends when we find the gift in it.

EXILE AS BOON

Boon means gift. The rite of exile is complete when we consider exiling as a gift. It doesn't mean we want to live in exile; few of us do. The only humans I know who choose to live in exile are desert mothers and fathers. Yet what is true about rites of passage is that we cannot live in any of them; we are always moving through them. So bless your wailing in the desert, your Creator who allowed you to keep wailing until there were no more tears to weep.

Exile is over.

You may be lucky enough to return to your tribe or, for me, the red tent, but you never fully return once you have earned the rite of exile. You are different. Removal will surely come again, but you will know how to submit to it now. You will remember there is a gift in the silence waiting for you. Silence is always waiting for us, but our work is to be in it long enough to receive its wisdom.

As you continue walking unaccompanied, you are comfortable in the silence. Silence has become your friend. She helps you hear your inner self when the world gets loud. The rite of exile ends when you see the red tent in the distance; you see the women's silhouettes moving around the premises, actively about their work. You realize you have left the haven of exile. They will be waiting to receive you. You will be given time to tell of your accounts in exile. They will also need you to help, for you have been missed. Someone spots you from afar, and it is the young ones playing outside the tent. They begin yelling your name as you draw closer; they announce your completion of the rite of exile. One of the wise mothers comes out of the tent and greets you with a silent embrace. Her arms are knowing; you stay in her embrace and let your bodies greet each other. You feel her body listening to yours. Finally, she releases you and looks you in the eyes. "Welcome back, beloved."

Exile is over when we find others who can embrace us.

HOMING ANEW

The exhaust from our minivan filled the carport as I ran cough-
ing, arms filled, half dressed, to join my three waiting children in
the car. *Damn. We are always late for school.* Three more days
until summer break, and I mentally cheered myself to press on
as I happened to smell my armpits as we reversed down our
driveway. My children's conversation couldn't drown out the
most recent elementary-school-shooting news report swirling
around in my head. As we pulled up to the school, I let my body
memory walk my kids to the front doors. They were locked. We
were late again. Moving halfway through a school year is never
easy, but the twenty-minute drive to this new school was different from our prior three-minute drive back west. I don't do well
with time. The door buzzed open, and I signed the kids in. I
prayed under my breath as I watched them walk to their classrooms. I wondered if I was the only parent who was scared to
death to drop off their kids at school. I knew only four other
moms by name, and I imagined I should call them and ask. As I

walked to the car, my thoughts ran wild. It wouldn't be until I shut my van door that the weight of anxiety filled my frame.

"I can't do coffee this morning. I need tea," I said aloud to no one.

I drove to our coffee shop and ordered my tea. Locals filled the space, and I recognized a few people by face but didn't know their names. Again, I felt the cold, angry slap of loss. I longed for my coffee shop back home in Seattle, and I felt every bit of the two thousand one hundred and ninety-three miles I was away from it. *This town was not my town, and these were not my people.* I had no desire to chitchat; my inner world was louder than I could bear. I went back to my van. I shut the door and let the silence envelop me. My anxiety had been building all week. Dropping off my kids at a school that still felt new, where we didn't know anyone. There were no familiar faces as there were in our Seattle school morning rhythms. We were still strangers here.

"Oh, I know this feeling. I need to cry." I continued to counsel myself out loud in my empty van.

I didn't want to cry in my car on Main Street, but I was relatively new in this town and didn't have many friends I could ask to cry in their kitchen. After a few minutes, a friend came to mind. I texted her.

She immediately invited me to come over.

As I stepped into her sweet, welcoming home, I felt hot tears prick the back of my eyes. *Speak fast, Christy,* I thought. *Don't overwhelm her.* Instead of seeming overwhelmed, she continued vacuuming to clean up the morning mess from breakfast, and I didn't hesitate to speak over the hum.

"Thank you for letting me come over. With the school shooting, I had trouble dropping the kids off at school today."

Tears were welling up at this point; she turned off the vacuum, and before I let one tear drop, I blurted out, "Can we pray?" The tears poured out, and she would have had to be a monster not to say yes. Luckily, she loved Jesus and had been a pastor for years. So there in her front room with her dog and her vacuum, she didn't hesitate. She moved me toward the cozy rug in her library.

"I like to kneel face down when I pray about things that bring tears." She knelt on the rug, lowering her chest to her thighs and her face to the floor, and motioned for me to join.

I smiled and knelt beside her. We prayed for peace for school workers and students all over the world. We let our mother-heart-sized tears anoint our prayers for our children and the children in every elementary school. I felt relief and peace creep in as we ended our prayer. Her husband walked in and was surprised to see me and his wife kneeling with their dog, but he was kind and joined our conversation about pastoring a world holding so much grief and fear.

I left their home that morning with some relief. The rite of exile felt like it was coming to an end. It is brave to walk through exile but even more courageous to build anew after. When we move toward others and offer them our vulnerability, we create a bridge amid our hearts and receive a moment of reprieve.

RITE OF
CREATION

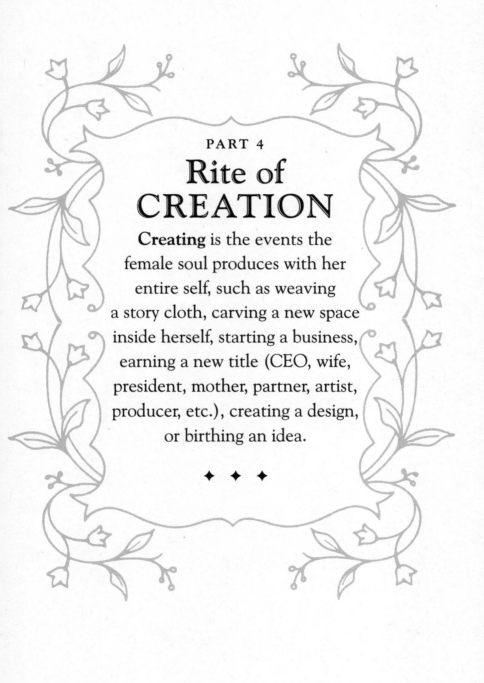

PART 4

Rite of
CREATION

Creating is the events the
female soul produces with her
entire self, such as weaving
a story cloth, carving a new space
inside herself, starting a business,
earning a new title (CEO, wife,
president, mother, partner, artist,
producer, etc.), creating a design,
or birthing an idea.

◆ ◆ ◆

WOMEN ARE CREATED FROM BONE

Women were created intentionally. Women were created by God, on purpose, for a purpose. Genesis 2 tells us that "the Lord God formed man of the dust of the ground, and breathed into his nostrils the breath of life; and man became a living soul," which God called Adam, meaning "from earth" or "from soil." God then took one of Adam's ribs and with it fashioned a woman, who was to be called Eve, meaning "mother of life."

Now let's tell the story with a little more imagination. Before the biblical story of Eve's birth, the Talmud and the book of Isaiah refer to Lilith, which some have understood as the first woman to live with Adam. Jewish myth states that Lilith was Adam's first wife, a woman made from dust just like Adam, and was in constant conflict with him because they both came from the earth. The story says that the Creator decided that Adam needed a better partner and put Adam to sleep, taking a bone from his rib cage and creating Eve. Her name meant the mother of life, the female created from bone rather than dust. The spiritual work Adam must do involves the story of his own origin, the struggle with the ground, while the work Eve must do involves her own unique story, the struggle that will take her back to the body.

Too often, the church gets stuck in theological conversations about whether the story of Eve coming from Adam's rib cage suggests a woman's submission to her husband. I hardly think that is the point of man and woman's creation story. Instead, it is that women are made from something very different from what men are made from. The female does not inherently struggle with the earth, rather she struggles with the body. Women's bodies are telling us a story. The bone, the flesh, and the body are what Eve was created out of—a woman's glory and shame come from a power and war with her body. Thus, I look at the female's bone structure and her organs to help me understand her armor and the story she tells with her body.

While women have the exact same 206 bones as men, I want to focus on the female's clavicle and pelvic bone. Particularly for the female body, these two bone structures are skeletal gateways to the throat and the vagina. If you were to fold the female body in half, just above the navel, the throat and the vagina would lie parallel to each other. The average lengths of these two canals on the female body are 3.5 to 5 inches. These two passageways both lead to an opening: the throat to the mouth and the birth canal to the vaginal opening. Both of these openings are protected by a rim, either the mouth's lips or the vulva's labia. The women I have come to counsel in my practice have stories that usually involve one of these parts of their bodies being targeted. Often in the church, a woman is silenced for speaking out or because of her sexuality. This highlights that where a woman creates life from is often the excuse for a woman to be singled out. The mouth produces words and the vagina brings forth life, both the human viability and the sexual sentience. Women's bodies were created to speak through their voices, their sexuality, and their bleeding. God created the female from bone and breath. The Creator gave her a vagina and a throat, two passageways from which to produce—this is the female's rite to create. The rite of creating is when women use their bodies to create in all forms of expression: word, ululation, empire, stillness, song, book, orgasm, poetry, film, baby, partnership, growth, marriage, play, singleness, and love.

WHEN WOMEN BLEED

Scarlet red. Topaz gold. Russian violet.

These painted colors of blood flow from the women depicted in the art piece I have in my bathroom. My husband bought it a few years back from a local artist. The image is both mysteriously and boldly painted. The women are black silhouettes seated across from each other with brilliant colors of menstrual blood cascading down in a rainbow-like river. So, of course, I am both unnerved by and drawn to the image. Women's blood is not a "beautiful" topic, but it is also their most potent compass when creating.

Creating is the very essence of the female. Every day, women make without even choosing to: our bodies create breath and circulation, our minds create thought patterns and ideas, and our choices create systems and future generations. There are three steps when we make something: planting, tending, and producing. In my book *Theology of the Womb,* I say that the female cycle is to bury, wait, and give birth.

My friend Rebecca has become dear to me in our first year in our new town. Her kids match up well with mine. She is a delightful, honest, and authentic human. Our families have tried to make a weekly meal together and have done so somewhat successfully. This particular afternoon, I met up with Rebecca to walk before picking up our kids from after-school music lessons. I never made it out of the car. Rebecca's eyes were red when she greeted me: "I spent a lot of money buying T-shirts and DISARM HATE pins from Everytown's Moms Demand Action." We ended up talking in my car for the hour while Rebecca cried and cussed and ate most of the chocolate bar I had brought for us to share. Another school shooting was making all of us mothers crazy with uncertainty about how to respond. Rebecca was brilliantly inspiring in this moment of craze, yelling, crying, and hitting things. Despite my own fear and anxiety, Rebecca's holy rage made me feel alive and ready. I blurted out, matching the crazed look in her eyes, "It makes me want to be at the kids' school every second. If someone is going to come in and kill them, I want to be with them!"

Often when I volunteer at my kids' school on Wednesday mornings, I walk the halls and pray. Recently, after the shootings, I've pictured myself running straight at the gunman, catching every bullet by throwing my body on top of the shooter, bringing them down. In that imagined moment I feel fearless. The truth is I have no anxiety about what I would do if I were there; I only fear that it will happen when I am not on school grounds. It is the powerlessness to control the situation. A mother feels cagey and ruthless when her young are being targeted.

I rolled up the windows of the car because someone was in the parking lot. We were both yelling and crying now, two mothers uncertain of any other choice we had in this moment but to listen to our bodies.

"I'm also on my period. I feel like I am bleeding so much this cycle." I knew the feeling: women's menstruation flow is affected by hormone levels, physical activity, stress, and even weather. For example, cold weather constricts blood vessels and is believed to impact menstrual flow, increasing period pain. While these are all physical impacts on bleeding, I believe there are spiritual and emotional situations that are congruent with our period flow. In a spiritual context, I believe women bleed alongside the Creator in solidarity. **Women's blood is their most honest outrage.** I actually believe that when my body menstruates I have the courage to say some of the most profound truths. Some of my most honest prayers to God happen when my body bleeds. I reached over and put my hand on Rebecca's shoulder. We cried out in tears to God to have mercy on our children, our schools, and asked for direction in how to faithfully respond. Then we collected ourselves and picked up our aggregate of six children and decided to meet up in an hour and have a family dinner all together.

As I was driving back to my house it dawned on me that Rebecca needed a bubble bath. I called my husband and asked him to be on dinner and kid duty so that I could create a protected space for Rebecca to relax. I felt exhilarated as I cleaned out all the hair and kids' toys in our Jacuzzi bathtub. I got candles, fresh towels, chocolate, and drinks and filled up the bubble bath with Epsom salts. While I felt very excited, I was nervous. *What if she doesn't want this? Maybe Rebecca will say no. Am I ridiculous for offering this? What if we aren't this close of friends? Is this too weird for a forty-year-old woman to be offering to their friend?* Even with all the thoughts running through my mind, I womaned up and marched into the kitchen. Rebecca was cutting raw chicken and helping my husband prepare dinner. She greeted me and I blurted out, "Do you want to make my dreams come true?" She laughed out loud and said, "Sure." I had her wash her hands, led her to the bathroom, and told her that I would work on dinner and watch her kids for the next half hour. She accepted the bath and texted her gratitude later that night.

This is the work of creating—to risk honest lament and radical care for our friends. When women's bodies bleed, our most honest thoughts and needs come to the surface.

HER CREATION

I googled "the greatest first lines in masterpiece books" when writing this book. Reading through the first sentences that formed some of our literary masterpieces was a wild and exhilarating search. "It was the best of times, it was the worst of times," Charles Dickens begins, or Lewis Carroll's "Alice was beginning to get very tired of sitting by her sister on the bank, and of having nothing to do." Then I thought about the Bible, the most printed book ever written, and quoted the very first line out loud.

"In the beginning, God created."

The first recorded act of God in the Bible was creation.

Mother God creates from her infinite self so that each creation is like no other. No snowflake is the same as another, no leaf is the same as the next, and no meal is cooked exactly as the one before, no matter how closely you follow a recipe. Each dish is to be experienced as it is during that exact place and time. Tasting is about the present. Creating is about the present moments collected in one place.

In Psalm 139, the psalmist says to God, "You wove me to-gether when I was in my mother's womb."

God created a world with an ecosystem that sustains life-forms. God created humankind that can procreate itself. God is a creator. Period. God uses women's wombs to give women a front-row seat to the rite of creating. Please do not limit this to carrying a baby, or you will miss God's lesson about creating. Yet the legend of the female existence has often been reduced in patriarchal cultures to cooking, cleaning, having sex, and child-bearing. But the rite of creating is much more than domestica-tion; it has gotten lost in translation over time.

Sitting in my office with clients, week after week, I hear the same complaint: *All my husband wants from me is to cook, clean, and have sex with him. He leaves his crap on the floor or dirty dishes piled on his nightstand. And even though I work part-time and care for the kids, he expects me to look like the actress on TV.* Now, I know this is not every couple, but so often, the female soul is dried out living in domestication without vision. She inherits a history in which the men were hunters and gatherers, and the women raised children and cooked. This system has been passed down and is limiting the female imagination. Women internal-ize this crippling heritage in their bodies, knowing they were created for so much more. This belief system also sets up men to believe that their only worth is in providing.

Once the patriarchal, evangelical church took hold of this belief system, mistranslated a few Bible verses, and began preaching it from the pulpit, women had few options. They could choose to submit and support such an oppressive system, or they could rebel and be ostracized. These limited and unim-pressive choices caused many young girls to figure out how to engage with a world that tells women they are only as important as their bodies look. A longitudinal study from New Zealand showed that *women who live in objectifying cultures die eight to ten years earlier than the female life expectancy worldwide.* Again, women die eight to ten years earlier when they live in a society that believes that female bodies are objects, not human souls. God never created the female body as an object for speculation or insertion. The woman's body was crafted to create.

Women have power that they are afraid to own. In the United States, women have 85 percent of the spending power; women spend $15 trillion annually in the United States and $31.8 trillion globally. Ninety-two percent of women tell another woman about a product they like.

✦ 93 percent of women have consumer power when buying pharmaceuticals.
✦ 91 percent of women have consumer power when buying a new home.
✦ 93 percent of women have consumer power when buying food.
✦ 92 percent of women have consumer power when purchasing vacations.
✦ 80 percent of women have consumer power when choosing healthcare.

Women have so much more power than we take authority and accountability for. It is time to spend our strength in productive ways. When women take back their power and use it with conviction, we will turn this world around for the better. Sadly, many women are still stuck in archaic systems, believing their capacity to create is met by having a family and kids. Women get exhausted by cooking, cleaning, and having domesticated sex. Yet the wild female soul is always in there, dreaming and scheming a fantastic story she longs to live. Creating is about cooking and weaving—cooking up ideas and weaving dreams that will make this life unforgettable. If you think the work of cooking and weaving is domestic, you have never been taught how to cook or weave. God, the Creator, spent many of Her days knitting and cooking all of creation.

WE ARE IN HER KITCHEN NOW

"... you should try our blackened catfish and chocolate soufflé, which Mary Sheppard was known for."

The young, white waitress didn't seem very knowledgeable but gave every customer this recommendation. Yelp agreed with her advice, so I ordered it and added the fried green tomatoes for apparent reasons. I am not a cook, but I do love to eat. And when in the South, and when there is a woman of color offering her food, I gladly say yes because the Good Lord Himself somehow shows up in that dish. Happy with my order, I return the menu and look across the table at my friend, ready to talk about all we had just seen in the last few hours. Middleton Place has become a landmark for thousands of mothers who have left a legacy for women that we can all learn from.

"How did you find this place? I have so many feelings."

A few weeks before, I was hesitant when my friend Autumn invited me to meet her in Charleston, South Carolina, on a rice plantation once occupied by one of the highest numbers of enslaved women in the United States. Middleton Place is now a gorgeous historical hotel hosting tours and events for racial reparation. I am always a little uncertain if I want to go to places like this because, historically, Arthur Middleton reluctantly signed the Declaration of Independence for South Carolina. Plantation owners did not want more than 40 percent of those they enslaved to be men for fear they would overtake the enslaver. Because Middleton Place was a rice plantation, most of the work could be done by women, whom enslavers did not fear. Autumn and I had just finished the tours of Middleton Place and felt gutted by the vast number of unknown deaths and cruel treatment.

I longed to know more as I walked through rooms with walls covered with women's names without any information about who they were. We did, however, find some hope that present-day Middleton Place holds annual reparation weekends for Black and white descendants to come together and share stories and meals. As a woman with spending power, I want to support places of historical oppression in the work of repair. Unfortunately, the United States is so far behind in our work of racial reparation that white people must be intentionally investing in places that promote healing.

Next to the pictures of the Middletons was a picture of Mary Leas Washington Sheppard, the head cook for the family. The plantation renovated the kitchen into a restaurant that sells Mary's most popular dishes. We were eager to get out of the South Carolina heat and into an air-conditioned restaurant serving her legacy recipes. Edna Lewis would become the famous cook, Mary's protégé, helping her carry on the secret recipes. When people asked for a recipe, often there was no way to explain it because many enslaved people couldn't read or measure; they would cook by smell or taste. Wood-burning stoves precluded measuring temperatures, and so people relied on sight or feeling.

Long after these women died, their meals allowed us to meet them. It is not uncommon to get to know a chef through their dishes. The way something is cooked holds meaning. Oppressed women had to learn to execute their ideas through intuition and experience. This is the work of the present-day woman who has lost her way; she must learn from Black mothers and grandmothers to create from the strength within. In the recipes, we can hear what they are teaching us.

COOKING DOWN MY ANGER

One of the reasons that I never learned to cook was because my grandparents had a plantation in the South, and their help did all of the cooking and cleaning. It is a part of my story that is more complex than can be written about here, but explaining where I learned about cooking feels necessary. There were three women whom I loved deeply: Mary, Eola, and Autherine. These women worked in my grandmother's kitchen every day, and I spent hours sitting on the counter listening to them teach me about cooking. I was nine, watching them prepare our lunch. Eola was a boisterous Black woman shaped like a cushioned macaron, who could cook like a Michelin Star chef. I was helping her clean the collard greens, and she was cutting them a certain way, explaining that you must put all your hate and anger into these challenging greens. Her Creole Cajun dialect coached me in the kitchen: "Collards are the worst greens in the garden, an' often slaves had to figure out how'da make the worst food scraps delicious." I watched her use every part of the greens and put them in the wrought iron pot.

"How much longer, Eola?" I would ask every thirty minutes.

"Them are stubborn greens, Chrissie; they needin' alotta time to soften, just like you and me."

We giggled as we waited; we would move on to a different dish to prepare. But before we started, she would envelop me in her soft embrace. I loved her hugs, which lasted as long as hugs should last. If I close my eyes, even decades later, I can still feel the warmth of her body, the way she would laugh when I was in her embrace, and my little head would lie comforted on her bosom. Then, she would turn to the next pot and have me stand on a stool pushed against the counter; she would coach me to hold a spoon in one hand and scrape the remaining cream from the corncob into the bowl. I hated this job; flecks of corn juice would spray in my face when I didn't press down hard enough. Yet this was one of my favorite dishes. Maque choux is a Creole French corn dish I make yearly in the fall. Thirty years later, when I scrape the cobs, my hands can almost feel Eola's hands coaching mine. When I was young, my weak hands weren't pushing down hard against the cob, so that I couldn't produce the petite cream, the best part of the secret ingredient in the recipe. Instead, Eola repositioned my spoon and pushed hard on my lazy hand. Working so hard for such little scraps seemed so pointless. I can still hear her Creole French accent clear as day.

"Aw honey, you ain't never gonna get anything out unless you work harder." So she would say as she shook her head and made this ticking sound with her tongue. I knew that sound; it was the kind scolding of an elder correcting the younger generation. "That's what is wrong with your generation . . . you throw away the most important parts 'cause you never learn'd the best part is in what you call the scraps."

We talked little because it was hard to understand Eola's Creole dialect, so she often communicated with her body and her cooking. It seemed like hours would pass before I sat in front of my steaming dish of collards and corn, a dish I loved. The maque choux melted in my mouth, like many flavors dancing the perfect dance across my tongue. The bitterness of the greens was not tart or offensive; it was honest against the sweet bacon. The meal was a gift of nourishment and comfort; there was no detection of hate. Eola was the mother of thirteen children and worked for my family's plantation her entire life. She was one of the greatest creators I knew. Her spirit left a legacy of an open invitation for racial reparation. For me, she did that through her cooking. She spent countless hours of her life in my grandmother's kitchen and her own kitchen, teaching the world that we must be patient as we cook down the anger of injustice in this world. Little did I know that years later, long after Eola passed, I would think about resilience, survival, and injustice when I cooked.

When my parents split up, my dad had custody of my older siblings, and my mom raised me and my younger sister. In a matter of months, we went from very wealthy to very poor. My mom had no money. I spent most of high school working two food industry jobs; I worked the drive-through at PJ's Grill and waited tables at the local seafood restaurant. I was always picking up odd jobs when I could, like working for a friend's mom filling king cakes during Mardi Gras season from ten P.M. to one A.M. No matter how much I worked, I always remembered coming home to my mom sitting at the kitchen table, bills surrounding her, and me contributing what would never be enough to pay them. I watched my mom crawl up from the lowest place when my father divorced her. She went from being a stay-at-home mother to working full-time and attending night school. Most nights, dinner consisted of me and my little sister digging through the pantry for something to eat because my mom spent her evenings away.

Although I was in middle school, I only knew how to make two dishes: collard greens and a "maque choux" corn dish. We rarely had fresh vegetables in the fridge so I would make up a game at dinnertime for my sister. She would close her eyes and I would sneak into the pantry and match two canned vegetables that seemed to pair well together. My mom always had cans of corn stocked, so I would grab corn for my base and then another random can that didn't seem too terrible. I would come around the corner and tell my sister to open her eyes. I would yell, "Corn-soufflé surprise!" and she would clap and cheer and we would set to work on making dinner. I miss those moments cooking with Eola or with my baby sister. It was never about the food we were eating; it was always about being together. Food is about sustenance but a meal is about connection. Cooking is the recipe we know in our bodies that creates a table where all are welcome to gather.

SETTING THE TABLE

"Where should I put these?" my uncle is asking as he strains to hold up the crystal vase holding a hundred yellow roses.

There are only a few table settings I can remember in my lifetime. The most prominent one is my great-grandmother's table at her hundredth birthday party. One hundred white linen napkins, rose-embroidered china plates, silver cutlery, crystal glasses, and hand-painted nameplates at the top-left corner of each table setting. One hundred guests had been invited. The one hundred yellow roses that filled a crystal glass vase were placed as the breathtaking centerpiece. I was a teenager and excited to be invited to the table. Although it was a glorious setting, and one hundred people had been chosen to sit at the table, I was aware of those who weren't. In the kitchen, handfuls of helpers busied themselves over serving each of us.

Jesus washed the feet of all He invited to His table. When we set the table, we must understand that it is our job to serve the guest who comes. When we make others do the work of cooking and serving, we haven't set the table, and we are just hosting an event. There is a place for everyone—to host, cook, set the table, clean, partake, and cultivate the space.

We must notice who is not being invited to the table. Men and women need to realize that the table was created for everyone to have a place. The kitchen is not a place for one gender, especially not for people of only one race. The legacy of women is a movement that can exist only if we all are invited to the table, each taking turns at the head of the table. Young girls must learn how to cook and set the table from their grandmothers, learning the heritage of femininity that all are welcome and all bodies are to be nourished. These cooking lessons are not only about food. These lessons are about the cycle of envy and forgiveness, the work of rupture and repair, and the nourishment and preservation of the table.

Let's be honest about my table for one hot second; it's a mess. My dining room table is ninety-five percent of the time covered in my children's stuff. There are paper clippings, art scraps, Play-Doh crumbs, and often paper plates with leftovers that my husband and I were too tired to make our children clean up. Sadly, in my home, that is where our parenting skills fail us. My husband and I joke that whoever goes to work is lucky. For years, we swapped, one of us staying home with the kids while the other showered, dressed nicely, stopped to grab a coffee from a coffee shop, and went to work to discuss their problems with grown adults. We would come home to a partner who had stayed home with young children, wiping poop, making meals, and, occasionally, cleaning the house. The table was often a visual representation of how the day had gone. Even now, I don't fully understand the gift of setting the table, but I recognize those who do.

I was teaching at a women's retreat for three days in Tennessee. It was the first time my colleagues and I had put money into hiring a Christian couple to cater and host the meals throughout the retreat. Jessica and Jeff are a farm-to-table, bring-heaven-to-earth kind of couple with the gift of deep and abundant hospitality. Each morning I would wake up to Jeff cooking a gourmet meal, and every evening, as we prepped for the next day's events, Jeff was there late into the night, chopping and cleaning. While I must acknowledge that he could do that because his wife Jessica went home to put their children down to sleep, my body felt their service to us in such a healing way. Finally, the night before our retreat ended, all thirty of us drove to Jeff's farm-to-table private kitchen for a special dinner. The night's landscape and sunset were breathtaking, but as I turned to find our outdoor dinner seats, I saw that each plate had tableware settings, cloth linens, glasses, flower arrangements, and handwritten cards.

The table was set for queens.

The table is a way of curating an experience. We underestimate the gift of the table setter, the divine wisdom it takes to bring the power of the feast to the individual. The table is referred to seventy-six times in the Bible. Jesus used the table as a place to find sustenance and strength, a place of communion and to share food and conversation with loved ones and enemies. The one who sets the table is doing far more important work than we have named.

The following morning, I felt a "glory hangover." Not a hangover that involved alcohol, but rather the feeling I have when I am dizzy and exhausted from the goodness I consumed the evening before. Jeff and Jessica had wrecked me in a good way. I did not want to return to my crap-covered table at home. They inspired me to have reverence for the table's significance and honor what it offers, to come to the table and be both welcomed and held. I snuck downstairs before sunrise to grab some coffee and prep for my final teaching. Jeff was there brewing a fresh pot. I thanked him and tucked myself into a chair facing the lake for a sunrise view. As I jotted down notes, I could hear Jeff tinkering in the kitchen, and tears began to slide down my cheeks. Curiosity chased my tears, and I knew the tenderness I felt was unfamiliar.

In my time in Christian ministry, I had never been to an event where men served me. Never had I been paid to teach a gathering where men upheld the space and cared for me while I stood in a place of power. Now, I must be clear: my husband did that by taking care of our children every time I went on a work trip, but this felt different. So, I let the tears fall as I watched the sunrise, listened to Jeff clank around breakfast pans, and smelled bacon frying in the kitchen.

That afternoon, we ended the retreat with a marking ceremony. A time in which individuals took turns blessing themselves in front of the entire group. As the last individual went, I felt the tug to bless Jeff and Jessica publicly. We had not discussed it as a team, and I felt sheepish. The cooking staff was in the kitchen prepping our final meal. I snuck into the house and asked if they could come outside if they had a chance. When Jeff and Jessica stood in front of the crowd, I explained my experience growing up as a woman in the church. I told them about countless conversations I had with male authority that believed I should not be teaching or sharing from the stage. My tears began to expose the hurt place inside of me as I told them of my experience witnessing Jeff cooking and cleaning while I taught all weekend. I took oil and blessed Jeff's and Jessica's hands for their unseen and influential work of hospitality and care. Never had I felt so moved by the power of the table. The table this couple had offered me that weekend blew me away. The unabashed welcoming power of love and serving felt like Jesus had washed my feet and invited me to the table. We must all learn the power of a well-set and welcoming table. And the first thing we do to set a good table is choose our tablecloth.

STORY CLOTHS

"Alexa, play 'Follow the Drinking Gourd.'"

I turn to see my eight-year-old daughter has come into the sunroom to help me prep for gardening. I had never heard it and expect it to be some silly song she had learned from a school friend. After she calls out to Alexa to play the song, she states that we need to listen to it because it is almost springtime. The song is hauntingly captivating.

> Follow the drinking gourd
> when the sun comes back,
> and the first quail calls.
> Follow the drinking gourd.
> For the old man is waiting
> just to carry you to freedom.
> Follow the drinking gourd.

My daughter explains to me that when enslaved people were trying to find freedom, they sang this song as a road map to follow when the spring came. In school she had learned that "the drinking gourd" represented walking through the river and following the Big Dipper, which pointed north. Then casually she adds that in the South, Black people had to use the Green Book, which told them safe places to reside when traveling.

I was stunned that I did not know about these historical guideposts of American history. When I looked them up, I saw that she was correct. Jeanette Winter wrote the book *Follow the Drinking Gourd,* which is based on an African American folk song that tells the story of a peg leg sailor who taught slaves a song about the drinking gourd (the Big Dipper). Many used this song as an escape map, making their way north from Mobile, Alabama, up the Ohio River, and to freedom in the North. My daughter was also correct about the Green Book, which served as a travel guidebook for Black motorists from the 1930s to the 1960s to find safe places to stay.

"Isn't it so sad that people had to share songs and books to tell them where they could be safe?" My daughter's voice is incredulous as we toil through the garden bed pulling weeds. I explain to her that when people didn't have the freedom to publish books, they could only tell stories through secret objects. Our foremothers were teaching survival skills through their songs and story cloths. Ancestral quilts. Tablecloths. Treasured textiles. Social fabrics. All of these story cloths have been passed down with messages from our ancestors. Because our history documents so few women's lives, we must find the stories in the recipes and quilts passed down by our maternal ancestors. Recipes and story cloths were the only history books our foremothers had. Other than Mary Leas Washington Sheppard's award-winning recipes, Middleton Place had an artifact necessitated by infamous events, latent with deep wisdom, a story cloth. Story cloths are fabrics that encompass a story we can rarely read accurately in a history book. Because women were limited from documenting their accounts, the story cloth is a historical artifact. Sadly, we cannot know the stories just because we hold one of these story cloths in our hands. History is rarely written this way, but Ruth Middleton did it. She weaved the words in a cotton sack. In her book *All That She Carried*, Tiya Miles shares the story of Ashley's Sack, the cotton sack a devastated mother gave to her nine-year-old daughter before being sold into slavery. Here are the words of the story Ruth Middleton wrote:

> My great-grandmother Rose
> mother of Ashley gave her this sack when
> she was sold at age 9 in South Carolina
> it held a tattered dress, 3 handfulls of
> pecans, a braid of Roses hair. Told her
> it be filled with my Love always
> she never saw her again
> Ashley is my grandmother
> Ruth Middleton
> 1921

Without these words, there would be no account of this act. These words give a history to an entire lineage of Middleton women. I cannot fathom having to watch my daughter be sold, and yet this grieving mother courageously gave her daughter all she could to help her survive. On this story cloth we can see that Rose wanted her daughter Ashley to have clothing, food, and her hair, as a token of her love. As a sisterhood, our mothers are telling us how to survive through heinous loss and suffering. Our foremothers are calling to us, beckoning us to hear the message of survival written in their story cloth. I can hear their whispers—*Remember who you are, that you come from a long line of strong women, and you are loved.*

Womanist theology is the study of God through Black women's lives. Time and time again I have listened to Black women tell their story and I find myself in awe, like a student frantically listening to their mentor who has gone before them. The fore-mothers are telling the sisterhood that love is the only way to create amid hardship and loss. They are teaching us to create through knitting tightly together one another's stories to make a collective story cloth, the legacy of women. I am learning that to tell our stories we must learn to weave.

WEAVING

Standing in the beautiful Asheville Grove Arcade mall, I realize I am desperate for retail therapy. Sadly, there are better places to shop for clothes; the few clothing stores here are selective and expensive. My daughter wants to go to the yarn shop, and I comply, giving up any ideas of shopping for myself. There are exquisite colors of yarn, and I immediately feel insecure. I do not sew like my grandmother. I do not crochet like my great-grandmothers. And God knows, I couldn't weave something if I watched one hundred YouTube videos on the subject. When it comes to making my clothes, the buck stops here. Now my daughter looks at me, longing for beautiful yarns and a mother who can teach her how to clothe herself. I am not a woman who was trained in this skill, but I understand it. My feminist thoughts quickly want to shun the idea of sewing with my daughter. Yet, I have learned that women historically weaved, sewed, or knitted clothing. The Bible even mentions that the "perfect woman" sews clothes for herself and to sell; it even emphasizes, in Proverbs 31:22–24, that "everything she wears is beautiful."

The art of weaving is much larger than clothing, much like the art of the uterus is much larger than bearing children. The female is invited to these cooking, weaving, and childbearing tasks as more considerable conceptual demands on the resilience of womanhood. The female knows innately within herself how to create. Historically and today, the duties of cooking, weaving, and childbearing can be understood as physical tasks but, even more, as deeply feminine traits of creating.

Unfortunately, weaving is a forgotten art. The female body innately knows how to weave. But not simply incorporating material, weaving the world we live in. Yet if the female's body is subjected to shame, objectification, and self-harm, she will struggle to weave her internal world and external reality without honest grief and repentance.

"We are being given the opportunity to stitch a new garment, one that fits all of humanity and nature."

In her book *The Body is Not an Apology,* Sonya Renee Taylor refers to stitching a new garment, but not in the standard way we think. She explains that we have ascribed value to systems that confine us, but that weaving our inner journey with our external reality creates a tapestry of radical self-love. Radical self-love of our female bodies takes us out of failed systems of self-sabotage, body shame, and worthlessness. When the bodily hierarchy occupies the female body, she is not free to weave a tapestry that brings life. Females inherently create life-giving things. Although many women may choose not to make a human in their bodies, women are innate weavers. Weaving is about bringing one's internal feelings into an external expression. We can weave anything into a creation: a tapestry, a film, a human being, how our day unfolds, a meal we make, or a story we tell. Women, if we remember back to the idea of setting the table, we evoke a life-giving act of weaving. Preparing a meal is one of the most beautiful creations because it keeps humankind going. By weaving a conversation, food, and drink, people coming together at a set table create a tapestry.

CO-CREATING

While co-creating is a rite of passage in many ways, it is not mandatory. We co-create in friendships, our relationship with our parents, and, most plainly, with our partners. We invite others to knit with us. Weaving shows up in co-creating. We are commanded in the Bible to leave, cleave, and weave. This art of weaving is a gift we can teach our partners if we have learned it ourselves. We see with each couple that there is a pattern to the work they weave.

"Baumans, come over here for a second . . ." Mrs. Upton called us to the check-in window at our kids' elementary school. "Selah walked past the other day, and I was just struck by how beautiful she is, inside and out. All your children are just similar."

Andrew and I beamed like proud parents. Our kids do look a lot alike. They all carry our physical and spiritual traits pretty evenly. They feel like a quilt we have created, weaving honey-brown hues and expressive feelings tightly together into a family. While our children significantly represent what Andrew and

I have co-created, there is a larger pattern to our relational tapestry. We have a style of creating together. We usually like to split our work and play time pretty evenly—we work hard and play hard. For example, when we were engaged, my dad and stepdad each gave us ten thousand dollars for our wedding. With the first ten thousand dollars, we bought land in Africa for sustainable farming and a clean water source. With the other ten thousand dollars, we hired incredible photographers and musicians for our reception for hours of celebration. This co-creating theme has been carried out through our marriage; we split everything fifty-fifty.

Every relationship co-creates a pattern. While this is most common in partnerships, it can be marriage, friendship, and family, and even among co-workers. Some like to co-create in one specific medium: publishing books, painting art, hosting podcasts, summiting mountains, producing films, completing marathons, exploring cultures, learning languages, or writing music. Others like to dabble all over the place. Co-creating is one of the most exciting aspects of the rite of creating. It allows you to be known.

CREATING DEFINED

There is a pattern to all creating.

Creation is cyclical.

It moves from light to dark, winter to spring, and flood to drought. The cycles of creation are always the same: life-death-life. Making something mimics a similar process: sow, water, and reap; brainstorm, design, and execute; dream, invest, and collect. Creating is an act both inside of us and outside of our bodies. Creation is the magic of my body making something where there was once nothing. The female creates within herself and with another, which is co-creating. Co-creating encompasses the magical phases of birthing life and death with another, which is not limited to but can include anything from our thoughts, dreams, productions, corporations, publications, and empires, and our relationship to marriage, children, pets, estates, and legacies.

In lifespan therapy, we often begin with the origin, the story of our birth. For most, that brings us to our relationship with our mother and father, our initial definition of self-worth. As we age, we walk through the rite of initiation into adulthood; we learn the strength of our perseverance in exile. Then we find ourselves invited into creating. But because creating always follows the pattern of the life-death-life cycle, we can understand how to create only by knowing how to die. How we bury is an essential indicator of what will come from the soil in a new season, our intuition. The best guide through the rite of creation is one's intuition.

RITE OF
INTUITION

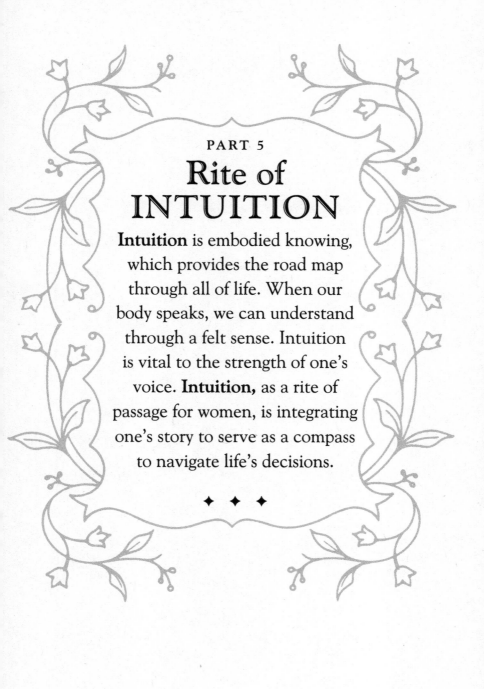

PART 5

Rite of
INTUITION

Intuition is embodied knowing,
which provides the road map
through all of life. When our
body speaks, we can understand
through a felt sense. Intuition
is vital to the strength of one's
voice. **Intuition,** as a rite of
passage for women, is integrating
one's story to serve as a compass
to navigate life's decisions.

❖ ❖ ❖

THE BELOVED WOMAN

CHEROKEE NATION, NORTH CAROLINA

Land of the Lady Braves

CITY LIMIT

LAND OF THE LADY BRAVES was printed in white, cursive letters on the city limit sign as we drove into Cherokee, North Carolina, for a camping weekend. My aunt Jinx and I were taking my kids camping on the Cherokee reservation and visiting the Native American museum and Oconaluftee Village as an educational field trip. This village was still practicing daily tribal life, not subject to state laws, and those who lived there spoke the Native Cherokee language. Story after story during our tour blew my mind about First Nation culture and history that I, in my forties, had not known. The Trail of Tears is the Native Americans' story of being pushed out by white settlers from their land. Once again, I had to find the courage to hold my white fragility and learn about a significant aspect of American history marred by systems of oppression. It was eye-opening and horrific all at once.

The Cherokee society is matrilineal, and the government is run by three leaders: the Beloved Woman, the Peace Chief, and the War Chief. The War Chief wore a red leather outfit with wild turkey tail feathers. The Peace Chief wore a white-and-yellow leather outfit every seven years when renewing the vow for office. As interesting as it was to hear about how the Cherokee society elected peace and war leaders for their tribes and honored those offices, it was astounding to hear of the essential role of the Beloved Woman. During ceremonies, the Beloved Woman wore a thick, oversize, sleeveless coat made only of wild turkey breast feathers. It was bold and not that attractive looking, but you could tell it held more power than all the others.

Honestly, I would have missed the whole lecture had my aunt not encouraged us to stay longer. My kids were restless, and I had only slept briefly the night before, camping outside in the cold air. So, when we were all ushered into a large, circular clay building in the middle of the village, which they called the community hall, I wanted to bail on the tour. Yet this entire culture being run by women fascinated me, and I ignored my sleep-deprived moodiness and grabbed a pen and paper to take notes.

The mud walls and erect center pole made the dark community room feel cool and welcoming. I stood awkwardly with an achy back as my two-year-old softly snored in the backpack I was carrying him in. This Cherokee community hall is used to discuss any needs of the village. Decisions are made as a community, never in solitude. Ultimately, if a decision cannot be made by the community, the Beloved Woman decides.

"She is called the Beloved Woman," the tour guide says, holding a hanger displaying a cape of wild turkey feathers, "because only a woman leader knows how to continue on the human race."

My head shoots up from my notes, and I stare at the unappealing cape of black and white feathers. The Beloved Woman was in charge of how anyone would be disciplined, fed, or adopted in the entire community. She led these decisions with a council of women that she chose to govern with; they were considered the rulers of the society. A panel of women was ultimately in charge of all the gardens, seasons' cycles, and matters of nourishment. The Peace Chief and War Chief would seek counsel from the Beloved Woman whenever they were unsure how to proceed.

Under matrilineal rule, everyone belongs. Everyone in the tribe has a purpose. The Beloved Woman, the War Chief, and the Peace Chief divided the tribe into particular clans. Every community should have a Beloved Woman. For some, this is a pastor, a friend, a Parent Teacher Organizer (PTO) mom, or a neighborhood activist. Every intuitive woman is in charge of her people. Whether you have been entrusted with a community, a child, a spouse, or a friend group, you have been invited to care for them. This is the work of the intuitive woman.

WE BELONG TO EACH OTHER

Beloved Women, intuitive women, know that we belong to each other.

We know that the humans most in need are as crucial as the human in the highest position of power.

The world is filled with Beloved Women.

Ella Josephine Baker. Amanda Gorman. Alice Walker. Edith Cowan. Julia Gillard. Vida Goldstein. Emtithal Mahmoud. Munnira Katongole. Meaza Ashenafi.

Seattle taught me how to think like a Beloved Woman.

Ijeoma Oluo. Nikki McClure. Robin DiAngelo. Nancy Murphy. OVW-WomenSpirit Coalition. Brenda McNeil. Karen Schneider. Ferntree. Hayden Wartes. Munyi Shea. Tina Sellers. Nyaradzo Mvududu. Bethanne Kinmonth. Angela Tucker. Katherine Douglass. Coté Soerens. Sparrow Carlson. Cher Edwards. WHEEL Women in Black.

These women are just a few who held up the torch to show me the way. Women just like me, who are pastors, activists, mothers, shamans, wives, professors, coffee shop owners, authors, law writers, truth tellers, and artists. Each one of these women sees humanity in the eyes of others. During my time under their tutelage, I was in awe of how they continued to point me to the eyes of people who are orphaned, unhoused, domestically abused, bullied, sex trafficked, and addicted. I have listened to these women from church pulpits, sidewalk megaphones, lecture halls, coffee shops, kitchen counters, classrooms, and the steps of courthouses.

There is one group of women whose actions both haunt and comfort me even years after, the WHEEL organization, whose members dress in black and stand on the courthouse steps every month to represent those who have died unjustly or alone on the streets of Seattle. These women embody the heart of the Beloved Woman who has been entrusted with all her people, those orphaned and those who belong. The Women in Black stand there holding a poster board with the names of those who died, and for those whose names were not known to anyone, the women write the term UNKNOWN and hold it up to represent the human who died unnamed. These women have no idea who they are holding the poster board for. They are simply women committed to mothering in the way the Beloved Woman teaches all women to live. I know many mothers, some of whom have lost relationships with their children due to estrangement, addiction, or abuse. Some mothers do not know whether their children have run away or been captured. My children are young, and I cannot imagine such a world with one of them estranged from me to the point that I don't know where they live. Yet thousands of unhoused humans live in Seattle. When I pass the tent cities or see someone standing in the street, I now think, *That is someone's child.* The Women in Black have taught me that we belong to each other, which means that every human living on the street is somehow connected to me.

Before living in the Pacific Northwest, I didn't realize how many biases I had. I mentally had a judgment for every person I saw on the street. Because our church building was on the road with the most sex-trafficking in Seattle, I saw so many things that I never saw going to a brick megachurch, whether the half-naked women I drove past on North Aurora or the unhoused men paying for blow jobs in their shady vans. It wasn't until I started going to a church that served these congregants that I realized I had learned little up until that point in my life about how to act like Jesus. I became part of the worship team for a congregation whose mission was the neighborhood with unhoused and sex-trafficked people.

One Sunday morning, I was taking the trash out before church, and my husband was feeding the kids breakfast. I saw Pedro's van parked on our street as I rounded the brick corner in my bare feet, eager to get back inside. I waved to Pedro, and his eyes met mine with shame. Then I saw Catt, a woman who worked the corner, exiting his van. I was surprised at my embarrassment. But Pedro came over to our house, hung out with our kids, and I guess I hadn't put it together that he paid for sex. I knew most of the men we ministered to paid for sex. I quickly shut the trash can, nodded to both, and returned inside. Communion that day at church was awkward at best. Pedro was standing next to me when our pastor instructed us to break bread and pour grape juice for each other. I averted my eyes from Pedro's as I watched his shaking and dirty hands break a piece of bread for me. I couldn't think fast enough whether it mattered if he had washed his hands since this morning's activity. He interrupted my thoughts with the words "The body of Christ." I mustered all my strength to receive the bread and wine while whispering, "Thanks be to God."

Before I listened to my intuition, I bowed quickly to my judgment. I made opinions about who was Christian enough, clean
enough, modest enough, or educated enough. It wasn't until I
came up against street-smart people that I realized how many
biases I had consumed. My judgment might say Pedro is not
holy enough to offer me communion. Whereas my intuition
might say the body of Christ was sacrificed and His blood was
shed for everyone, sinner and saint. Which is why we pray,
"Lord, I am not worthy to receive you, but only say the word
and my soul shall be healed." Intuition says Pedro's dirty hands
were covered in the cleansing blood of Jesus. We are all children
of God and we belong to each other. God said Pedro is worthy,
the Beloved Woman says all are worthy, who am I to say differently.

PADDLEBOARDS AT DARK

"Do you want to meet a few other women and me at Green Lake on Halloween in witch costumes to ride our paddleboards across the lake?"

I stared at her as if she were not a well-respected theologian on my doctoral committee. My mouth was agape in shock, as if she had asked me to tag a federal building or rob a grocery store. *She wants me to do what now?* Ask my husband: one thing I am not is a rule breaker. Technically, this is not illegal. It is just wild. Growing up in the church, I was taught to run away as fast as I could from two sins: sexuality and mystics, or, spoken in hushed tones, witches. Women who did not follow the pious way of God. Yet when my mother returned to Catholicism, her devotion to reading about every saint opened my eyes to women of wild and passionate faith. I began to hear story after story of women. But at this point, I had already bought into the lie that powerful women in the church were not to be revered. God could not be both male and female. Eve was not to be discussed except for the "forbidden fruit" faux pas. Mary was spoken of only at Christmastime and with care not to make her an idol. In seminary, I knew a good sermon about a female character in the Bible would not be admired. Sadly, I believed and perpetuated the patriarchy.

Despite my judgments, my passionate and fanatical mother continued to tell me of these great saints. On summer break from college, I relented and read *The Interior Castle,* by St. Teresa of Avila, which carved deeper grooves into my awareness of the health of my soul. The new saints kept popping up every time I returned home for a visit, and my siblings and I made a game of it. What new saint would Mom be praying to this time? We could pray to St. Clare of Assisi for protection from television and computer screens or to St. Kateri Tekakwitha, the first Native American Catholic saint, who is the patroness of ecology. Looking back, I made fun of it because I inherently believed I could follow only men in the Bible when it came to God. As I began to experience more of the world through a female body, my faith grew too large to be contained by only stories of men. I craved a God who created me, a woman, in Her image. Yet I knew that was heretical in my circles. Suddenly, my mother was more progressive in her gender-inclusive beliefs than I was in mine.

Women's stories began to teach me about a God I had never comprehended. The spirit of the female was wild, dangerous, and alluring to my soul. I began to study the women in the Bible with more fervor. I read books on female saints. And then, some might say, I went to the dark side and read *Women Who Run with the Wolves.* Every bone in my body began to pulsate so loudly that I could almost feel the blood cells circulating from my marrow. Clarissa Pinkola Estés was my initiator, and her stories initiated me into womanhood. There were few people I could tell in my Christian circles that I was reading her work and any story of mystics, witches, and death doulas. Even my husband, my boyfriend then, cautioned me that if I was too "woo-woo," no one would trust anything I said. The problem was that I had never felt so alive as when learning about this stuff, and it made me love Jesus more than ever. But I was getting my master's degree in seminary, and a reformed seminary at that. The discussions with my old, white professors looked a lot like this.

> **Me:** Jesus loves women.
> **Professor:** Of course, easy.
> **Me:** The female is made in the image of God.
> **Professor:** Sure, I guess that's true.
> **Me:** God created women in Her wildness.
> **Professor:** I'm not sure we should use "She" for God.
> **Me:** God transcends gender.
> **Professor:** Hmmm . . . I have to think about that one.
> **Me:** *Then we can learn something unique about God from all genders.*

Intuition is when we speak for ourselves from within our integrated selves. These seminary debates became a place to bring my voice to be the author of my intuitive story. While I never had the honor of talking about my wildest Christian thoughts with those seminary professors, I learned I didn't need to give anyone authority over my relationship with Christ. Only God gets that power. And God is more significant than all of us think. Never has God felt threatened by the books I read or the training I push myself to experience. Instead, God made the female with a knowing sense that I have the utmost confidence in.

INTUITS BECOME INITIATORS

The rite of intuition is the beckoning of an initiator. The initiators are the women who take our breath away—the women, as the author Sue Monk Kidd refers to them, who have taken their own breath away. What do I mean by all of this? Have you ever taken your own breath away? Have you ever done something so far outside of what you thought possible that you were in sheer awe of yourself? The initiators are the women in their fifties and sixties who lived these lives. Initiators are the women who, when you stand in the room with them, make you blush at the thought of them noticing you. The initiators are women like Supreme Court Justice Ruth Bader Ginsburg, who was known for her revolutionary work against sexism and advocated for equal pay, or Sally Ride, who became the first American woman in space and went on to create science and engineering programs specifically for girls. Virginia Apgar, a qualified surgeon, was discouraged by a male head doctor from practicing because she was a woman. Virginia persisted and became an anesthesiologist and created the Apgar score to test a newborn's health.

These are initiators—women who persist in the face of adversity and take their own breath away. When the younger generations witness women who have lived their fullest story, girls want to become women.

When girls are initiated into womanhood by these kinds of women, they become teenagers like fifteen-year-old Claudette Colvin, who didn't give up her seat to a white woman just because she was African American and inspired Rosa Parks nine months later to make the same choice. Or twenty-two-year-old Amanda Gorman, who read her incredible poem "The Hill We Climb" at President Biden's inauguration. Diana Taurasi, a California high school basketball player of Argentinian and Italian descent, became a WNBA professional athlete and five-time Olympic gold medalist. These girls were fearless as they persisted in the possibility of becoming women who made a difference in this world.

Who are your initiators? Who are the women in your life whom you look up to? What women's lives have permitted you to dream bigger than you ever thought possible?

For me, bringing people laughter felt like a luxury at first. As I have aged and the world has grown more serious, I realize that laughter might be the most expensive medicine we can buy. There is another initiator I learned about recently, Moms Mabley, an incredible teenage girl who, after the loss of her father and a sexual assault, became America's reigning Black comedienne. There is something so unbelievable about a human who survives hardship and then offers the world laughter.

I remember flying home from a conference I taught at. I had enough money by then to order myself a cocktail and a charcuterie board on the plane. For so long, airline flights without kids were an uninterrupted time for work, and I would often write nonstop, but on this trip, I wanted to watch a show and relax. There was a tribute to the ten most revered female comedians who changed the world for women wanting to pursue a career in comedy. I was mesmerized watching this. These women were hilarious, but even more, there was a strength to them. They gave the gift of laughter to others. Sometimes, it is harder for a woman to be lighthearted and a jokester because we carry so much in our bodies. Yet here were these women carrying the torch for female comedians. After the show, I wondered if there was ever a time in my life I had thought it possible to be a comedian for my profession. Definitely not. My family had pounded it into my head that I had to get a college degree, maybe multiple. So, I became a therapist—the opposite of a comedian. Yet I wish I had even thought that my career could have included any of the following: comedian, professional athlete, astronaut, or president. They weren't in my repertoire of ideas. Most of us cannot dream of what we cannot conceive as a possibility.

The rite of intuition is to become the storyteller, the initiator for those being initiated. Remember, the rite of initiation is the first time we learn something for ourselves. The moment we try something we didn't think possible and see that it can become our own. Yet the rite of initiation can happen over and over again. It cannot be contained. The rite of intuition calls forth all the midwives for the next generation. The knowing woman calls forth the younger.

GRAY IS FOR GLORY

"Do you like the gray? I decided it was time to go all gray. It might take me a little bit to get used to."

Her words were not foreign to me but hearing them aloud was nice. An aging woman naming aloud the bind of her body, shifting to a different stage of life. She continued discussing her body's climacteric.

"If the acceptance of gray isn't enough, a lot of wrinkles are added to my body."

My client wasn't old, but who was I to say? Age is about how you feel. In truth, she had done a lot of Botox, and her face looked flawless and frozen from her twenties. At times, it can be hard to work with less-aware women who have done a lot of cosmetic alteration to their bodies—it numbs a part of them that we often try to access when doing holistic work. Most women in my office get Botox on their faces to reduce wrinkles and feel better about their aging appearance. This presents a dilemma for the therapist who often uses the face as a compass for their client's story. My husband says, "The weathered face tells the best stories. We need those wrinkles to read our clients' most courageous moments."

The human face has forty muscles with six significant pathways to the brainstem and the rest of the central nervous system. Because Botox blocks nerve endings from sending pain signals to the occipital part of the brain, it can positively and negatively impact our psychological health. For example, where Botox is known to lessen traumatic memories through blunting one's neurotransmitter systems, it simultaneously can be detrimental to other cognitive domains. This is neither good nor bad, but it can present a block for the female doing integration work. Picture using your body as a map for your level of self-knowing, and the compass is your face. While your entire body can give you intel into your life experience, your compass has some blocks. When exploring our intuition, we use our story as the guide. When we alter our bodies, it is as if the GPS on one's phone gives fewer routes than possible. Our integrated bodies match the present moment. When our face freezes in place attempting to resurrect the face of our youth, we cannot offer the world or anyone in it our most integrated self. My client was staring at me, tears brimming in her eyes, but her face remained perfectly set. Her gray hair was breathtaking, but the tears showed she was grieving her aging body. When I asked her about her emotions, she replied quietly, "I can't stop death from coming for me. I am getting older by the minute, the second. I will never be young again."

The first shots in the war with the aging self can be fired earlier than we think. Aging is the standard progress of psychological and physical decline, the inability to adapt to metabolic stress, and senescence. In my book *Theology of the Womb*, I talk about senescing, the last stage of the womb, the season of growing inward or down. We will talk about this more in the rite of death and legacy, but the passage of intuition is the acceptance of senescing, the decline of aging. My sweet client was faced with what every woman who has grown up in an objectifying culture has to grieve, the invisibility that comes with aging. In a world that worships external beauty, the female's body's natural progression past her prime will leave her in a battle she can never win. We will all age and must mature from the objectifying culture's immaturity. The female's beauty has much more to do with her wisdom, depth, intellect, and heart than her appearance. This cage we have put ourselves in has a key: maturation. Intuition understands that aging is an invitation to a more complete, more encompassing portrait of the female. Intuition also makes us initiators of the next generation of women, but sometimes they get stuck in their jealousy of youth. Here are some levels of initiators:

+ **The Beauty-Focused Initiator:** She is trying to "stay young" by keeping her physical appearance as young as possible so that she can be desired by those being initiated. She is committed to spending all of her time filling any wrinkle and counting every calorie.

+ **The Fearful Initiator:** She is reading every headline, studying every hoax or scam to find out how to protect her children and grandchildren. She is so afraid of death, loss, imperfection, war, etc., that she doesn't know what else to do except prepare for the worst. So she hoards food and water and tells her kids to.

+ **The Wild Initiator:** She makes little sense to the outside world. But she is full of wonder and mystery. She scares people with her unknowing delight. She mimics Clarissa Pinkola Estés's Bone Woman, as she knows the way to sing women's dry souls back to life, but she is unkempt and witchy.

✦ **The Balanced Initiator:** She balances birthing some of her greatest last-of-life dreams while passionately inviting the younger generation to join and create. Finally, she has space to be curious.

✦ **The Out-to-Lunch Initiator:** She cares nothing about anything, she has given up hope on the world. She spends her days busying herself with nothing but keeping herself busy. She doesn't risk her own life or anyone else's. She has opinions but never takes actions.

A DRESS FOR THE DEATH DOULA

I was standing outside of my favorite clothing store in our small town. Martha, the owner, seemed to put an outfit just for me in the window every month or so that I could not resist trying on. Often it was too small or didn't fit me pleasingly, but often enough, it was perfect. It was usually from Free People, a brand that seemed also to have a pulse on my style. On this day, it was a rust-colored jumper that I could not stop staring at. Sadly, it was too snug when I tried it on, so I moped through the store in case something else reached out to me. Finally, I passed a black, puffed-sleeve dress. In the back of my mind, I knew I didn't need another black item in my wardrobe, but I pulled it out to inspect it more closely. Finally, there was a sense that I should try it on. It had a friendly, comfortable fit and pockets. It was not a statement piece; it was practical. A black dress is helpful for every wardrobe. I asked the attendant to put it on hold, and I planned to come back the next day with a belt or two I wanted to try with it.

I forgot the belt, of course, but I was back in the dressing room with it the next day. It was like a whisper of intuition that said, *Buy this dress.* I get the same sense when rushing through Target with a vast shopping list flooding my brain, I pass the tampons and think, *Buy them.* It usually isn't a day later that I start my period, and if I didn't purchase the tampons, I go to Walgreens between clients to grab them. This is similar to this black dress. So I stared at my reflection and took a breath, and paused. *Buy this for Mema's funeral.*

As strange as it sounds, at this point, I am convinced the rite of the intuitive woman is becoming a death doula.

"Death doula" can be such an abrasive term. Offensive even— until death came. Again and again. My son's death. My sister-in-law's death. My grandparents' deaths. My father-in-law's death. Funerals required me to think about death. In the middle of a very liturgical Easter Sunday service, I realized the work of death doulas was a job done by women in the Bible.

Four women, each named Mary, stood near the cross as Jesus took his last breath. Salome and Joanna were mentioned as having helped prepare Jesus's body, placed him in the tomb, and found it empty on the third day. How have I been a theologian for years now and never seen Salome's and Joanna's names? These women were followers of Jesus, yes, of course. But we cannot overlook that they knew to stay with Jesus until his last breath, and they knew how to prepare a body after death. Some theologians speculate these six women already had the oils, herbs, and fragrances on them at Jesus's death.

Death doulas are a role historically filled by the "eldest daughter," the one who was often encouraged to become a nurse and therefore expected to take care of her parents at their death. Present-day death doulas are end-life caregivers who specialize in being with a person at the end of their life, curating one's experience at their deathbed, and preparing the body for burial. Death doulas are replacing funeral directors, as they feel called to mend our distorted relationship with death. They are often women who practice spiritual and feminine beliefs based on natural life cycles that require decay and rebirth. The rite of intuition is when women age out of fearing death and rewrite their definition of a good death.

INTUITION DEFINED

To intuit means to contemplate. Intuition is often defined as an instinctive feeling rather than a rationale. The work of intuition is integration. When women are integrated with their whole story, they can live intuitively in their entire bodies. The intuitive self is the woman who can know something immediately, without recourse to conscious reason.

Intuition is the development of our intertidal cycles. Intuition is the quiet, steady energy of "the knower within," who guides us about when to wait, run, hide, or show ourselves, do, or be. This distinction is learned in the soul place rather than in the cognitive. Our stories get invited into the knowledge of deep intuition, and we either deepen our internal knowing or stay in our previous knowing place. Our soul's home is our body, and our intuition is the compass. The most important journey in our lives is to return home. Intuition is the knowing we are born with but often forget over time. We must return to our story and reflect on it, resurrecting what we have always known.

It is not uncommon in therapy for me to ask a client to bring a picture of themselves as a child. We often can see in the face of our younger self our truest self. The deep wonder or awe we had for the world before trauma and loss stole from us. Intuition is knowing what is most true even if it is not evident.

INTUITING THE INNER CHILD

The inner child is one of my favorite therapeutic frameworks. One of my first therapists made me take my "younger self" on a date. I was living in the armpit of Central Florida at the time, waiting to get into graduate school, and my life felt pointless, so of course, I started seeing a therapist as any good Gen-Xer would. The humidity hit my entire body as I pushed the door to leave my therapist's office.

Take my inner child on a date?

What does that even mean?

In this worthless season of life, I had few joys, but I was proud of the cherry red Jeep that I called "Tullah," which I had bought when I landed my first full-time job outside of undergrad. With tearstained cheeks, I unlocked the Jeep and sat in the scorching-hot, Florida-sun-filled car, uncertain of what to do next with this assignment.

I exited my car, opened the passenger side, and pretended to let my inner child get in. I remember saying sarcastically out loud, "Okay. Buckle up. Where do you want to go?" I looked over at my empty passenger seat, feeling like an idiot, and I very clearly pictured myself as a six-year-old. I imagined she was begging me to take her to Claire's boutique in the mall. I hadn't been to Claire's in over a decade, but I drove to the nearest mall and walked in. I looked around the shop and saw the cheap, sparkly, colorful jewelry and hair trinkets. Trying to stay open to the exercise, I found myself drawn to a fluffy-purple-hair-topped rainbow pen. It was a ridiculous pen, but I knew instantly my inner child wanted it. So, I bought it.

Once I opened up to the exercise, the date with my younger self became effortless. We listened to country music all afternoon, played basketball at the park, and swung on the swing. I reflect now on how transformative that therapy exercise was. It had to be the moment I met my younger self again and thus completed a more integrated version of myself. A part of me that I only had access to that afternoon. As Carl Jung has termed it, the inner child archetype links this internal child to past experiences and memories of innocence, playfulness, and creativity. It offers us hope for our future because we remember the hope we had in our young selves. As you become more aware of your intuitive self during this chapter, be curious about your inner child and how you might spend more time getting to know her.

INTUITION VIGNETTES

She corrected herself without my invitation. "I don't know what I think— Ooh sorry, I mean, I don't know what I *feel* in my body." I tried to lead my client a little deeper into the work. "Let's try a little inner child work. We can start with nondominant-hand writing."

Sarha was reluctant but took the clipboard with paper and a pencil.

I acknowledged how weird it could feel to do nondominant-hand writing but continued to guide her. "With your dominant hand, write down three questions you would like to ask your younger self. It can be anything, like: *What is your favorite color? Does Mom or Dad like you? Who is your best friend?*"

She looked at me skeptically and wrote three questions with her dominant hand. I proceeded with the instructions. "Now, put the pencil in your nondominant hand and take the next five minutes to answer the questions."

Sometimes, I grab paper and pen and do the same exercise to ease the awkwardness. Then, I write out a few questions to ask my own inner child—which is to say, my intuitive self—what my experience is of my client's inner child. After a few minutes, her writing slowed, and I ended the exercise. "When you are finished, take a deep breath and put your pencil down. How did that feel for you? What were some of your answers?"

Sarha shook her hand as if it had started cramping. "I used the same questions you gave. I wrote down that my favorite color is purple, but my favorite color is actually blue. My favorite color was purple when I was a little girl."

SHE STARED AT THE SECOND sentence and began weeping as she gazed at the poor penmanship of her writing. Finally, she was barely audible when she muttered, "Mom hated me . . . and Dad liked me too much."

We paused for her to be with her sadness. My continued silence invited her tears to come fully. We sat together, held by the vulnerable energy and the sound of her grief. I repeated her answer after her tears had subsided some. "Mom hated me . . . and Dad liked me too much." The session was now under way.

Although we went on to talk about her relationship with her parents, we focused on how her inner child was hard to access without deliberate exercises. First, we worked on giving actual terms to the relationship she had with each parent. Her mother hated her because her father delighted in his little girl much more than he did in his wife. Her father was her surrogate spouse, and he used her to give him what she was never meant to give him. We began to unpack why her body immediately reacted to certain types of women and men. She wrestled with concepts and struggled to integrate her inner child's experience of her parents with her present-day experience of the people she met.

The trauma we experience, particularly with our primary caregivers, informs how we learn to engage in relationships cognitively rather than intuitively due to fear of misinterpretation. My client didn't trust intimate relationships with women because her mother was jealous of her from the beginning of her life, and her father showed more delight and interest in her than he did in his wife. Although we have already discussed misdirected delight in a triangulated relationship, this exercise focused on understanding how far my client was disintegrated from her inner child and, therefore, her intuitive self. She did not want to hear what her inner child knew about her relationship with her parents.

CLARISSA PINKOLA ESTÉS TELLS THE story "Sealskin, Soulskin," a parable about the cost of staying away from yourself and out of your soul skin for too long. When invited into a rite of passage, we get stuck but need help moving through it thoroughly. If our rite of passage gets hijacked by a relationship, such as an unhealthy tie with our mother or father, an abusive relationship, or our hatred of self, we never complete the passage. Historically, in all forms of hijacking or being stolen from, seven years is usually the maximum duration a person can stay stuck without completely withering away. When accessing your intuitive self fully, have you gone into a psychological slumber? How can you be freed to return fully integrated with yourself? We often see a lack of older women teaching younger women the path back to the intuitive self, which Estés calls the wild soul. Because of this, we must decide to undertake this challenging work ourselves, even if we have yet to be shown how.

The first step is to break from the mother, father, or lover that keeps us from being free. Then, we must turn toward ourselves and parent ourselves, promising never to leave ourselves alone. Next, we must commit to remaining integrated and mothering the parts of ourselves that have been orphaned and have become strangers to us. We must return home to our Mother of Intuition. Homing is the act of using our bodies as a map to return to our intuitive selves.

Rarely have I ever seen someone not be affected by inner child work. Often my clients begin resistant, yet the inner child usually wants to be heard and appreciates the therapist's demand to listen to her. While a date with their inner child or nondominant-hand writing does a decent job of introducing a client to their younger selves, it is just the beginning of the intuitive work for women. Once she fosters an integrated relationship with her younger self, she must integrate with her own body's story. This type of bodywork becomes a significant teacher as women learn to use their body's scars and stories to map out themselves. In the therapeutic world, we call this somatic work, which helps the body renegotiate events on a body-based level. Therefore, trauma-informed massage therapists, weighted blankets, ritual baths, and craniosacral work introduce touch to the body. With women horrified by the sound of those types of therapy, we begin slowly with body mapping. Body mapping works to identify scars, stories, energies, and errors that may be misaligned with the reality of the client's body. Objectifying societies have conditioned women to believe their bodies are objects rather than image bearers. In a day and age where antiaging is the top-selling type of product for women, the female has to work hard to stay connected to the reality of her body. We have forgotten the art of reading our body's map, which connects us to our intuition and guides us to the most integrated self.

BODY MAPPING

"Are you finished?" my voice quivered as I strained to look down at my fellow student, black Sharpie in hand, bent between my spread legs.

It was our first weekend intensive with my cohort, and our professor had us do body mapping. I had filled out body maps in my chiropractor's and massage therapist's offices and with my naturopath. In medicine, whether internal, muscular, or skeletal, we always try to map out the body. It turns out we also need to do this in psychology. In graduate school, my professor lined the classroom floor with butcher-block paper, and we took turns outlining each other's bodies and mapping our emotional scars from the story of our lives. It was life-changing. Before my eyes, I could finally see the invisible emotional stories that had scarred me. I took this into my therapy practice, often asking women to complete a body map.

Client: "I just got my kids all into school and now my husband wants me to go back to work to pay for him to go to graduate school. I feel something deep inside of me that is unseen, angry, misunderstood, and lost. I feel like I do not know what is mine and what is his or what is my children's."

Me: "It sounds like you feel resentful and like you haven't had a chance to catch your breath in a long time?"

She was weeping. She told me how tired she felt and that she had lost herself along the way to motherhood. My client explained that she felt unimpressed by the job of being a mother or a wife. For ten years, she told me, all she did was clean her house and care for her husband and children. The exhaustion was apparent on her face, and the anxiety had reached a new height when dropping her kids off at school. I knew that she had seven pregnancies and only three living children. I knew she had buried twins, her four-year-old son, and had had a miscarriage. As a therapist, I wanted to give her an opportunity to map out the story of her body on the paper. I asked my client if we could draw her body map. She agreed, and I pulled out a massive block of butcher paper and let it roll onto the floor. She lay down and traced her body's outline in marker. We stared in silence at the shape, and then I asked her to map out the story of her body with words, symbols, color shading, or even physical scars. She took the jar of colors and began to write comments on various parts of her body. She drew a black X over her left breast and six names over the stomach area, three marked with red X's. She wrote two men's words and one phrase over the vagina area. She continued with deliberation. She wrote her mother's name over her mouth. She finished the drawing with tears falling from her eyes, wings coming out of her back, and roots shooting down from her feet.

I stared at the image and became curious about what I didn't already know about my client's story. I asked her how she felt about her body map. She surprisingly responded, "I feel proud of her . . . she has survived a lot."

My client's body map was a road map to us all about what she has endured and survived. It was also a guide to remind her of who she was, intuitively, before the trauma. Body mapping can be done at any time in a woman's life, and it serves her to continually do this exercise as a guide to deepen her intuition. Integration of the exiled, creative, traumatized, or exhausted parts of a woman is a long journey filled with deep breathing and rooting herself repeatedly into her own story.

The sage-femme is the wise woman. Sage-femme is a French term used to describe the midwife. As we have discussed, midwifery is not only for births but also for midwifing death.

Our mind, body, and soul are all informative in aiding our intuition. When we walk through the rite of intuition we reflect upon the interplay of our stories and our bodies. As we age, our wise selves are integrated into our everyday thoughts, conversations, and dreams. The rite of intuition is another stitch in the fabric between birthright and legacy.

RITE OF
LEGACY

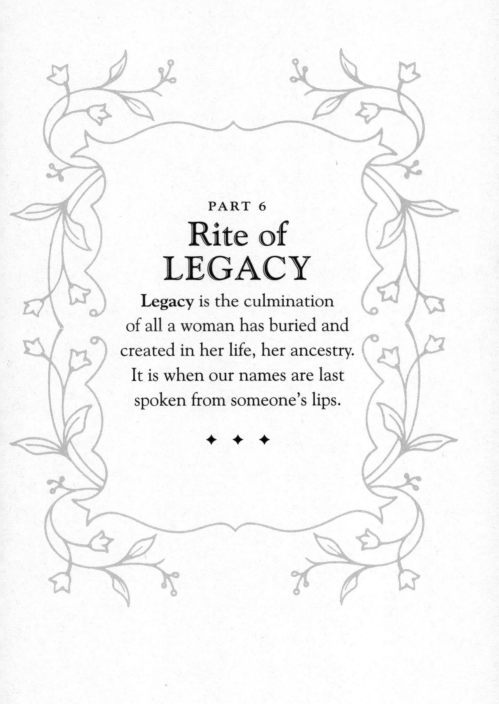

PART 6

Rite of
LEGACY

Legacy is the culmination
of all a woman has buried and
created in her life, her ancestry.
It is when our names are last
spoken from someone's lips.

◆　◆　◆

THE NIGHT BIRD STILL SINGS

I want to do something splendid . . . something heroic or wonderful,—that won't be forgotten after I'm dead. I don't know what, but I'm on the watch for it, and mean to astonish you all, some day.
—*Louisa May Alcott*, Little Women

Nightbirde is a legend in our home. We were mesmerized when we first watched her receive the gold buzzer on *America's Got Talent* for singing her original song "It's Okay." After that, it became a common practice to play the YouTube video of Nightbirde's gold buzzer clip throughout the day, and no matter how many times we watched it, all five of us would stop and take it in. Finally, as the clip reached the last two minutes, I would turn from the screen and see each of my family's faces. The response was always tear-brimmed eyes, gaping mouths, or audible wonder.

A considerable aspect of the beauty of Nightbirde's performance is that her cancer is a massive part of her story. When she tells her story of near death, we all wait to hear the words she deems necessary enough to sing. Even though Nightbirde received the gold buzzer, moving her to the finals, she would never make it to perform on that stage. Instead, her life was cut shorter than it should ever have been.

We were all sad when she died. We heard her lyrics repeating in our minds, that all was okay, knowing that was her mantra to her death. However, we did not realize that her one hit song, repeatedly played in our home, was not her last. To our surprise and astonishment, a new song by Nightbirde was released one year after her death. She had recorded a song and had it scheduled to drop posthumously. We listened in sheer awe to every word of the new music, and somehow we were getting to see her after the grave. The song was equally enrapturing, with haunting lyrics showing us she wrote her legacy and penned it to music while there was still breath in her lungs.

"How You were my portion when there wasn't
enough. . . . My God did not fail / It's the story I'll tell."

Nightbirde continued to tell her story after her death, and I invite you to do the same. We die twice, once when our bodies return to dust, the second when our name is last spoken on this earth. On that fateful *America's Got Talent* night, Nightbirde introduced herself by two names, her birth-given name of Jane Kristen Marczewski, and then she introduced herself by her wild name. She told the judges, "But I go by Nightbirde when I sing." Notice what she was articulating for us. She used a different, more honest name when she created her voice in the song.

NAMING HERSELF

All of humankind is born from a woman's body.
She tears herself open to bring forth life
and yet grapples to birth herself.

Men inherit the rites that come with masculinity
and must work hard to lose them.
For the rest of us, we must earn our rites.
A woman is not christened with ancestral glory,
she must name herself.

Often this name cannot be known at birth,
it is most clear as we approach death.
An epitaph, a compass.
Her Goldenrod, which knows her truest name.

Our name is essential. Often our given name is different from our wild nature name. Our birth names often leave a legacy and legends with our outlandish nature names. Naming is one of the first acts of God. When the darkness separates from light, God names day and night.

In Wildman's *First Nations Version: An Indigenous Translation of the New Testament*, the names of every character are not what I grew up memorizing in Sunday school. Mary goes by Bitter Tears, the Holy Spirit is called the Great Spirit, and Jesus is the Chosen One. This version of the Bible allows the colloquial Christian to see that it is a dangerous work to interpret God's words in only one way. Language itself is fluid, a continual movement of words in hopes of awakening the wonder of our great Author. What has your Creator named you? There is a legal name that our parents gave us, but there is a more holy name we each bear. The wild name can never be fully articulated in our life or death, but it is amid the throes of life and death that we can hear our most authentic name discussed in the rite of intuition; we do the bodywork as part of the map of our stories. This reflection of the knowing body is like a song of intuition that informs us how to name oneself. Sometimes it is difficult to recognize that we have been called by a name throughout our lives that was not truly ours. This is when we must be bold enough to rename ourselves.

WHY THE CAGED BIRD SINGS

"Lisa, how are we going to start calling you by a new name at forty years old? And you want us to call you Sparrow now?"

I loved this woman, but a legal name change at forty years old was bold. I struggled to use her new name in conversations for five years. Sparrow and I belonged to a sisterhood of the most perfect 1980s names: Lisa, Christy, Melissa, Karen, and Heather, yet as we all age, these names no longer fit us completely. Particularly for me, as I began to create and name my creations, I wanted more from my name. So my first book deal was a public struggle for me to decide if I could go by another name, a new name.

I didn't do it.

I decided it was easiest to use my legal name. The idea of a pen name felt like I wouldn't be asking for the recognition I deserved, while my full name felt clunky and hard to remember for readers. Also, my maiden and married names are always reminders of patriarchy that I can't shake. So there was the name on my diplomas, marriage certificate, and passport. Ugh. I feel a little excitement when I see that name, but my heart quickens when I coax off my wedding ring and see the letters B-E-A-U-T-Y engraved inside the band. Who is bold enough to change her name from Christy to Beauty? That sounds ridiculous and unprofessional. But when I consider my most authentic name as Beauty, I can see the bravest moments of my life flash before my eyes: the moment I untied an orphan child from her Lithuania bed, or when I lay naked waiting to be cut open to meet my youngest son, the first clean water that was sprung and given to a village girl in Malawi—these moments, when I remember my wild nature name, Beauty, I see her yelling in labor, burying her dead with dignity, and rising to have more children after child loss. She roars, which makes Beauty so stunning, her wildness.

Our wild nature name is spoken when we birth. Her strength is illuminated in her face, and she sees her most authentic self. She must engage her name when she creates a moment in time, a dream coming to fruition, or a loss being birthed. When she knows her full name, she leaves her most significant legacy.

What is your wild name? To learn this, begin with your given name and explore the moments in your life that called you to something more outlandish than your legal name.

GIVEN NAMES INFORM LEGACY

"Oh sweetie, I was a Catholic, but I was a very charismatic Catholic."

My mom was sitting in a wooden rocking chair with her bleached-blond hair rolled up in a circular, metallic-blue brush resembling a small club from the Stone Age. The creaking from her rocker and the roar of the blow-dryer didn't hinder her from yelling the story of my time in utero across her bedroom.

"When I was pregnant with you, I would go to these Wednesday night prayer meetings. Everyone was speaking-in-tongues. I remember they prophesied over you, said you would be 'singing, coming in and going out, leading the nations in worship.'"

She had no idea how strange she looked as she leaned down over the front of the rocking chair to rotate her wet bangs into a perfectly rounded cone that she continued drying. My mother had always had a propensity for melodramatic belief systems.

"I told you God had a plan for you from the beginning. That is why I named you Christy Angelle; it means Christ Angel."

I rolled my eyes. *What a freaking setup; who wants the pressure to live under that name?* I tuned out whatever she said. I only asked the question because my therapist said I needed to do more in-utero work. Who knew the journey of self-awareness would be ongoing when I became a therapist? I was, at this time, a thirty-one-year-old woman trying to understand my relationship with my uterus. I put my hand over my expanded belly and cautiously prayed over my child. *God, please be near Brave as he grows.* I interrupted my mom's monologue and thanked her, telling her I had to lie down. Sometimes it was exhausting to be around my mother for too long, and I wondered if I would turn out exactly like her.

It would be a short five weeks later when I would be back home in Seattle, standing in my church with the congregation praying again for my son. Brave was forty-one weeks, and we knew he would come at any moment. I felt ready, or so I thought; I had written out a birth plan explaining that I wanted an epidural, good music playing in the background, and to coach Brave verbally when the time came to birth him. Yet birth stories, as some of us know, are complex and rarely happen as we plan. Two other friends in our church were pregnant, and I remember our pastor praying over all three of us to have safe deliveries. Then, two days later, my friend Mel had a complication and delivered her sweet Rachel Jane without any life. The next day, when I went in for my induction, there was no heartbeat. Brave had died. Seventeen hours later, in a dark room with one blinding spotlight, my tearstained eyes focused on the tiny pink-and-green swirl emblem on the hospital gown covering my shaking knees as I labored a breeched, lifeless child.

They never tell you how to plan for death at birth in birthing class. And why should they? Death and delivery shouldn't be related. We have no death plans for birth. I think it is because

God never intends for death to happen during childbirth. I prayed no prayers during that delivery; there was relentless begging for his life. Yet the moment I started pushing in active labor, I could not pray. I had to focus; all my attention and every fiber of my mental energy went to birthing him. I chose to birth the son God had given me, which God had allowed to be taken from me. The details of those passing minutes are blurry in my memory, except for one thing I did remember to do: coach Brave's body out of my body verbally.

MY VOICE SQUEAKED OUT INTO a tense but quiet room,

"Brave, you can do this,
    come my sweet one,
    I have been waiting to meet you."

My tears gave way, and my voice grew louder as I continued my mothering. I was aware that everyone in the room was wildly undone by my words spoken out. I knew he wasn't alive; he couldn't hear me. And at that exact moment, I thought I was saying all these words aloud to mother Brave, but now, I know I was mothering myself. Our most anguishing moments, the scariest part of any rite of passage, are just a mirror reflecting who we are. In our darkest moments, we find out who we are. Therein lies the answer to the entire concept of this sacred journey; it is not about what rites of passage we survive, but rather, who we become and how we mother ourselves as we pass through them. It is in these times that we get a glimpse of our wild nature and the moments that reveal our true name.

I am showing you in this story that our legacy lies in our truest selves. If I want to know how I will die, I must look at how I am living. While I don't know when or precisely the way I will die, I know how I will die. This story is a road map showing me the future. I will die coaching myself with the fiercest love, fervent hope, and bravest faith.

QUESTIONS FOR YOU TO CONSIDER:

1. How do you go about naming things that you create?
2. How do you coach yourself in your darkest moments?
3. What are aspects of your wild nature name and the legacy you will leave?
4. How will you die or plan to leave this world?

How you responded to these questions will tell me the answer to the next question: What is your rite of legacy? If you are ready to find out, pause, take a deep breath, point your fingers—tips touching, hands semi-cupped above your head—and dive in.

Everyone dies, but first, everyone must be born. The way you tell your story, the details you pen, and the intentionality you put into the rite of passages in your life are all indicators on your life's map. So, as you finish reading this book, you will have traversed from your birthright to your death. As you outline the rites of passage in your life, it will make up a timeline that illustrates the themes of your story. The markers over your lifespan that give you the most intel to the legacy you will leave.

LEGACY DEFINED

Legacy is awakened at death. There is a complexity to our legacies because we have no control over how they are interpreted after we die. In his famous musical *Hamilton*, Lin-Manuel Miranda says, "You have no control, who lives, who dies, who tells your story." The impact is a prominent part of a person's legacy. What we choose to be intentional about is often ascribed to our legacy. Some proverbs say you die three times: the first time is when you stop breathing, the second is when you are laid into the ground, and the third death is when your name is spoken among the living for the very last time. Our third death depends a lot on how our life intentions and choices are remembered. Preserving takes a lot of work. Legacy preservation is cultivated over a lifetime and contingent on the generations that follow.

In our neighborhood house church many years ago, my friend Jay preached on the legacy of French herbal liqueurs. The heart of its heritage is a guarded secret. "For example"—Jay held up the large glass bottle of green Chartreuse—"only two monks know the entire recipe to this spirit." There is no physically written recipe for Chartreuse. Each monk memorizes a part of the recipe to keep the elaborate liqueur alive. In the Chartreuse mountains six hours southeast of Paris, the monks guard the four-hundred-year-old manuscript that lists one hundred and thirty plants and herbs that make up what has been named the Elixir of Long Life. The recipe held secret since the 1600s is used now in a distillery in southeastern France, as the Carthusian monks learn to carry the tradition on to the next generation. If the practice of legacy preservation is difficult for an entire monastery to do, can you imagine what it entails for every family system?

The Vidrine side of my family has a small vineyard due west of the Chartreuse Mountains, just outside of Bordeaux. While the wines made at the Château Doisy-Védrines are much less known recipes than the chartreuse, the drink holds much meaning for me. The château or crest on each bottle tells a part of my family lineage. While there is no secret to the recipe, our family preserves its worth by simple acts of bringing the wine to family reunions. It is our ancestors who teach traditions of old to the next generations.

Just like the monks who held the knowledge of the herbs, it is the crones who know the wisdom of the female legacy. The most common archetype likened to an old woman is the old crone. The old woman is a beacon to all women, conveyed in stories such as "The Sinister Magician" and "The Wise Woman." She has no burden of primping or demands of youth, she is an antique, all-knowing within her very existence. Being crone-y seems alluring to me. Not at first sight, of course, but when no other options are left. When my skin has given way to sagging perfectly in surrender. When my world consists of only what matters. The crone's work is carrying on legacy.

My great-grandmother Mamere was an iconic crone of a woman when I knew her. By my fourteenth year of life, she was celebrating being one hundred years old. Mamere was still spry and unpredictable; she could touch her toes and cackled at each great-grandchild trying to do the same. Mamere knew how to cook by taste rather than with recipes. Her body knew how to run her household, farm, and land. Her instincts knew how to conduct family dynamics in such a way that legacy was a part of her every simple move. And when it came time to die, after saying goodbye to each of us, the old crone midwifed herself to sleep. When I look back at what she knew, I am smitten by the role of an old woman. A season in life that has little to do with outward matters but rather with navigating the work of preservation for the next generation.

For women, we need our grandmothers, the sage-femmes, and our great-grandmothers, the crones, to tell us the secret recipe and how to preserve the female legacy. Women's legacies are sometimes reduced to their children and the next generation, yet there is much more to their heritage. The world inherits life from women. Women leave behind regenerative ideas, organizations, humans, sustenance, etc. Historically, women have created schools and orphanages and educated generation after generation. They have created gardens and taught us how to harvest and cook, feeding others by perfecting recipes. Women have created mathematical equations to navigate the space race. Women have led suffrage movements to advocate for those held back by injustice, poverty, and ignorance. Women have given their bodies to further humanity, medicine, and science. We must acknowledge these women's contributions to our society. Eliza Hamilton, Dolley Madison, and Louisa Adams raised funds for fourteen years to construct the Washington Monument in Washington, D.C.; Katherine Johnson, Dorothy Vaughan, and Mary Jackson were NASA mathematicians. The suffragettes Emmeline Pankhurst and Emily Davison advocated for women's voices and led hunger strikes until the United Kingdom declared amnesty. Without her knowledge or permission, Henrietta Lacks saved over ten million people with her lifesaving HeLa cells, which today has spurred a demand to our government to bring justice and equality to our discriminatory healthcare system. Many women do not know the impact they leave behind. Many women are innately wired to give up their lives on behalf of another, and this act is not often recognized or rewarded. Who are the monks, old crones, and sage-femmes in your life? Their legacies are a recipe from which we can create. It is our duty as part of the sisterhood to preserve the heritage of female existence. We must learn to become preservationists.

PRESERVATIONIST

"You can have my last canned figs."

I stared at my paternal grandmother with suspicious eyes. It was apparent how this woman had lived through the Depression and managed to leave her great-grandchildren fully stocked 529s for their college funds. She knew that legacy preservation involved establishing wealth and value for many generations. Jacqueline Vidrine, or Memeem, as her grandchildren called her, was a genealogist by formal education but a preservationist by experience. I can always recall her doing two things: researching and canning. As a genealogist, she researched only my grandfather's lineage and published book after book on our paternal family's side. Yet amid all those books carrying my lineage, there is minimal mention of any women. In her early nineties, she had almost completely lost her mind, but in her last days, she gave me something of her maternal history, her very last jar of canned figs. This probably felt like a more significant gift than any financial inheritance I received from her. Why?

Because the only physical activity that connects me with my grandmother is canning food.

My grandmother meticulously saved absolutely everything. Every food scrap had a container to be stored in, every rubber band had a ball to be collected on, and every item had been labeled and categorized. Every year she would preserve all the food she could harvest. She pickled everything. Pickled okra. Pickled eggs. Pickled carrots. Pickled beets. Pickled potatoes. The grandkids made endless jokes about how many items one woman could find to pickle. The woman could preserve like few I know. This may be why she knew how to study genealogy, because the art of preservation was in her bones. Like all of us, we learn things from survival, and her survival depended on her conserving skills. Memeem came from a low-income family and had a mother who collected every shrub and plant in her backyard to make meals and health tinctures. She grew up spending hours canning food. She would plant the seeds, water the gardens, and collect the fruits and vegetables. Then she would peel, cut and quarter, and cook them. My grandmother would add spices and vinegar to vegetables, sugar and pectin to the fruit. After boiling the mason jars and the lids, she carefully filled them to just below the brim. Wiped the tops with a sanitized cloth and closed the lids tightly. I remember watching her do this in my childhood. We would carefully place the filled jars in a pot of water at a rolling boil until the covers made a loud popping noise to signify they were sealed and ready to be stored. This is why it meant so much when she gave me her last jar of figs. She was leaving me with her family legacy, the one she had inherited from her mother, my great-grandmother. After she died, it was not the genealogy books that I sat and looked at, it was the lone jar of figs that rested in my pantry.

During that season after my grandmother's death, there were

years of settling her will. Dividends, W-2's, lawyers, and online auctions of our family heirlooms were not uncommon topics in emails I received. While she was financially generous with her bloodline, she was frugal with her affection and love. How I will create a legacy has been informed by my ancestors. When I look to my paternal family tree, there are prominent beliefs on what kind of legacy should be left. There was a theme emerging as I looked from my ancestor's wine to my grandmother's canning; being a preservationist would ensure leaving a legacy. Yet it was more about a legacy of knowledge than of love.

A LEGACY OF GREAT LOVES

My father posted a Facebook post telling the cyber world that he had met the last love of his life. He explained that he had been allowed to love five women over his lifetime, and this woman was the last of his great loves. I remember staring at the confession of words on the screen and the picture of my father's long, tan arm around a blond woman who looked very similar to many of the women he had been with over his life. Looking at his smile, I wondered if he was somehow more capable than I was of loving multiple partners throughout his lifetime. I had been raised a Christian who was taught divorce was wrong, and my father's sexual escapades were even more a disgrace to the teaching I knew. But for a moment, I let myself wonder if I had been more open to the world, could I have had the excellent roller-coaster ride of having five great loves? I felt jealous that my domesticated, committed marriage would never yield me such experiences.

I closed my laptop and shook my head; I had to admit my dad looked happy. And he sounded delighted with how he had chosen to love so many. Sadly, I hadn't seen my father in a few years; we didn't spend much time together. He doesn't visit and has yet to meet all my kids. Somehow my father's capacity to love is limited. My grandmother used to say, "Sweetheart, imagine you are in a desert and thirsty when it comes to your father. You have an empty jug for water, and you see your father in the distance, but he only has a thimble of water to give you. He gives you everything he has, but it only fills your jug up a thimble's worth. So, you have to keep walking to find more water. It doesn't mean he doesn't love you; it's just that all his love for you only fills you up slightly."

For a long time, I wanted my dad to choose my siblings and me to be some of the great loves in his life. Yet I always came up thirsty, even in the seasons he tried to pick me. It seemed like all he had to give me was adventures, but never his whole heart. With my dad, we never had a relationship in the deep. My entire life, whenever I would visit him, there was always a woman there that he was more interested in than me. Once I married and had children, I longed for him to be a grandfather to them, but he was always playing tour guide to whoever was visiting him. I know my father has left my children 529s for their college funds, just like his mother left me. And yet, I wanted him to leave them a legacy of his presence, not of his money.

My children's laughter outside breaks my thoughts, and I enter my backyard and see my husband and three kids playing on the trampoline; they all immediately begin begging me to join them. I concede. I make my way into their made-up game and soak up the moment. It would have been nice to have four other lovers after my husband, but those would have taken me away from the incredible loves I have right here. I might just have more than five great loves over my lifetime. I am learning how to leave a different legacy for my children, different from the inheritance that I was given from the generations before me.

Unfortunately, my father tried to pass down to me what his mother passed down to him, a legacy that cannot be felt, only earned. The rite of legacy is larger than what we earn, preserve, or inherit.

INHERITANCE

"You are going to regret signing that paper. You just lost at least half a million dollars."

My dad's voice was incredulous and demeaning as my shaking hand signed the forms. I was and am not a rich woman, at least not millions of dollars kind of rich. *Why am I signing myself out of my inheritance?* My family has a long history of rupture. A great-grandparent dies, the estate is distributed, and sibling relationships disintegrate. Grandparents die, and the whole cycle happens again. I come from a family of divorce, which means I have met my quota of relationship loss. I was signing myself out of the inheritance because I didn't want to lose my relationship with my siblings. My dad was still uncertain about why I decided this, but I felt free. And what is the goal of life but to die free? It was sad that it was not worth going into business with my siblings and risking estrangement. Inheritance doesn't always come cleanly; it is often intertwined with other family members.

The U.S. Department of Labor reports that more than half of Americans leave an inheritance to their children. Unfortunately, the discrepancies are vast, as 30 percent of white families leave an inheritance compared to 10 percent of Black families, 7 percent of Hispanic families, and 18 percent of Asian, Pacific Islander, Native American, and other families. White families inherit five times more than Americans of color. My family contributes to these statistics. I inherited, from my paternal side, money, land, and racism. For so long, I worked to correct what my ancestors did not make right. They left a legacy I didn't want to inherit. Inheritance does not only mean coming into money or assets when a family member dies. Money received is a gift, and as Gene Edwards writes, "a gift is worn on the outer person; an inheritance is planted deep inside—like a seed." Inheritance is more than monetary; it is the inherited traits you receive from your family of origin. This might mean genes that make you more likely to get diabetes or cancer. Or inherited skin pigmentation, which allows you to tan or burn in a matter of minutes. Inherited traits can even be generational, passed down from generational ancestry. This might be your uncle's storytelling ability or your grandfather's chess skills. Or your grandmother's green thumb, maybe the women in your family's double chin. Inherited traits are sometimes impossible to alter.

How we come to understand inheritance is essential. For example, in my family, owning land was very important. My grandfather believed it was the only thing we could never make more of, so we inherited land from him when he died. As a woman, I had never owned the land outright. In my limited thinking, that was a man's role. I had always known that globally more men than women owned land. And I wanted to travel, and in my mind, I didn't think about owning property, building on it, raising a family, and leaving it to my children. Until I had children, and then I realized I, too, wanted to leave each of them a piece of property. I think it reinforces our story when we own property in our name. I am not sure I want to leave my children money when I die, but I know I will try to leave them each a piece of land. A place where I made roots, created memories, planted gardens, and walked the property. I want to give them a history that their body remembers, a legacy of the memories made on that land. As we talked about in the rite of creation, our female ancestors did not all have the luxury to pass down property to their daughters. Yet it is the spirit of a woman that needs no land, no money, nor article to be remembered. The female spirit is everbearing and therefore she leaves a legacy through her very existence.

As a woman, I want the entire female legacy to be an inheritance of her rite, that the existence of every woman is everbearing. Women are forever. The inheritance I want to leave each of you is the power to know yourself, to claim the spirit inside of you as your own. To breathe deep life into your soul only to watch it exhale glory. In this book, I hope you found a place where you belong. In the territory where our foremothers have spent a lot of time, may you see the roots they left for you to attach to and grow alongside.

Good woman,
may you dig your roots deep,
grow your branches tall,
and carry her rites to the next generation.

FINAL BIRTHDAYS AND FUNERALS

"This is the worst birthday. I thought I wanted to celebrate this way, but now I just feel terrible and so depressed."

I am a hot mess. Curled into a ball on our king-size bed, I complain as my husband shakes his head in disbelief. I should have expected forty-one to be a disappointment after the extravagant celebration of forty. This is also my first birthday away from my community. My close friends are, at best, a three-to-five-hour plane ride away. We had friends come over the weekend before my birthday, but now, on the actual day, I sit here feeling like everything is the worst. Birthdays are complex for everyone. Some of us don't celebrate birthdays, some have huge parties, while others might have an intimate dinner with a few friends. Whether you celebrate your birthday or not represents how you were taught to engage your birthday. Birthdays have always been a big celebration in our family. The birthday girl is permitted to semi-celebrate her birthday for the entire month. Excessive might be the right word to describe how I was taught to celebrate. This puts pressure on me as I age; each passing year is heightened with expectations that we know will always lead to disappointment. Yet every year, I try to hedge my dismay by planning something elaborate. It never works. In my story, grief is a part of my day of birth; in some form, grief is felt every birthday. The birth story gives insight into how much celebration and grief occurred when we were born. Commonly, even if a woman does not feel connected to her birthday, she feels similarities to the day she was born. Our body remembers, therefore we can assume on some level our bodies remember if we were celebrated or not on the day of our birth.

Often women might feel distant from their stories of birth. If they have had their own children, their bodies are preoccupied with their children's birth stories. As a mother, I make a big deal out of my children's birthdays; we have a family birthday dinner, where the birthday child chooses their favorite meal. During the meal, we recount and praise the child on their exact hour and the first minute of recorded life. Then there is a separate party planned for school friends, which includes cake, a piñata, and words of blessing over the birthday child. As I write these traditions, I can see that I am setting my kids up for the same disappointment I have come to know on my birthday. We inflate the celebration and do not acknowledge the sorrow. Every year we age, we celebrate another year of life. It is also true that every year we age, we grieve another year closer to the end of our lives. This grief is felt more acutely when we are older, or when someone has been sick for a long time. Marking our birthdays as we age requires more capacity to hold the loss with the gaining of age. The rite of legacy is guided by how much intention we put into our birthdays, particularly as we get older.

"My mom has always kept a funeral file with tons of specific details. So, we actually staged my mom's funeral as a surprise for her seventieth birthday party."

I stared at my friend Mel in disbelief as she continued to explain her mom's excitement after the weekend party. She described how some of her mom's closest friends flew in for the party, and everyone was instructed to write a tribute to her life. There were hours of laughter and some tears as longtime friends shared stories.

Our society aims to mitigate grief if possible. We have lost the ritual that comes as we honor aging. Death and funerals are equally as important discussions as birthdays and anniversaries. Funerals are the birthday parties we get to plan because we have no control over our day of birth. I am planning on having a funeral for a queen.

A QUEEN'S FUNERAL

Her body is without breath,
she lies lifeless on a wooden raft,
anointed with oils and covered in orchids.
In her hair is braided golden leather.
This is her farewell.
Those who remember her,
the way she smelled on a spring day,
or looked dancing on summer nights,
her delight was still contagious in their minds.
Friends are here now, sending her to glory.
With raised and flaming arrows,
they ignite her story in blazing glory.
For each has inherited from her something that can never
  be taken,
she loved them,
believed in them,
she had given them each the greatest of inheritance
when she taught them to love themselves.

I was scrunching these words on the bottom corner of my bulletin. "This is so amazing that we go to a church like this," my husband whispered as he slid a few papers stapled together across the table to me. I had just settled the kids into Godly Play and snuck into the coffee and conversation time our church has before service, and I was surprised to see the words printed across the top of the papers—"Advance Planning for Burial Service." Well, not my usual conversation at nine A.M., but our new church does have about 85 percent white-haired sages in the congregation. I settled in as Reverend Elizabeth continued to explain the great invitation our funerals hold. Again, I was perplexed and unsure that this was an urgent topic for me at forty-two years old, but off we went.

First, she addressed questions about the burial rites, the burial service, the burial plot, and the burial method. Immediately my mind went to a recent conversation with my ten-year-old son. We had passed a cemetery, and I told everyone in the car that I did not want to be buried in the ground but instead wanted a Viking's funeral. I explained that I would like Andrew and the kids to put me on a raft and shoot flaming arrows to ignite the entire float at sunset. I figured if Mel's mom had planned her funeral decades prior to her seventieth birthday party, I should give my kids a heads-up. While I was sure this was a noble desire, my son Wilder had a few stipulations.

"Mom, I am going to assume you will die when you are very old because I don't want to consider anything else. I am just going to let you know that my kids will probably be old enough to participate, but my grandkids will be traumatized if they shoot flaming arrows at your dead body," he explained. Andrew and I erupted in laughter. He was right. This just might be traumatizing, and death is already intense enough. We don't need to add more potential trauma.

"You're right, love. We will only do that if I die really late in life," I assured him.

So, I filled out my burial paperwork effortlessly at church because of that recent conversation. Reverend Elizabeth continued speaking about the critical timing between death and burial. She called it "the wisdom of letting someone go, when to mourn, and how to send them to glory." The reverend also explained that our funeral should tell the story we want to convey about heaven. We discussed music, place, and the people we wanted to present and speak to. I realized I needed to start making a file for this event because I love a good finale. I looked over to see Andrew writing freely on his sheet. He leaned over to whisper, "My funeral will be epic."

As the lesson continued, I began to imagine what it would be like to actually shoot flaming arrows at a dead body of someone I loved, and for my son, his mother's body—the body that birthed him, nursed him, comforted him through heartbreaks, and rejoiced with him in celebrations. Our bodies are sacred to our stories. So after church, when we got in the car, I told my son I thought maybe they should shoot flaming arrows at a raft of my favorite clothes instead. He looked at me and smiled, wiser than me in many ways.

"That sounds much better, Mom. Now you get it."

The rite of legacy incorporates our names, how we lived, how we loved, and how we take our last breath. While we cannot know when we will die, many of us hope it is with loved ones nearby or while sleeping peacefully in one's bed. We cannot orchestrate our last breath, but the funeral service is a ceremony we can plan for ahead of time. Our burial rites can be navigated by knowing our birthrights. While women do not have a way to change how they came into the world, what name they were given, or who initiated them into adolescence, we do get to say how we want to spend our birthdays as we age, and our funeral day. Birthdays and funerals are the days everyone focuses on you; they are the days marking a completion. Your funeral is the day you mark the rite of legacy.

THE INHERITANCE OF HER RITES

Her rite is to be everbearing.

Everbearing requires repeatedly cycling through seasons of initiation, exile, and creation. The work of the integrated female is that she must learn to mark the life-death-life cycle so well that she needs no map other than her body. The rites of passage in this book have allowed you to integrate your story as a road map of your best self. Who were you before you began this journey of reclaiming the rites of passage in your life? Do you remember that woman who started exploring her story? What do you know now about yourself that you didn't know before? You are the same woman, and yet you are now more integrated than before.

Now you have images to accompany these rites of passage that you have explored and reclaimed. You understand words like birthright, initiation, exile, creating, intuition, and legacy more thoroughly. You cannot look at your reflection in the mirror like you did before. Your bleeding, ailments, creations, and scars are now your life's road maps.

The life-death-life cycle is something you are familiar with and can apply in the years and seasons of your joy and grief. Reclaiming your story allows you to live in an integrated body that offers the world a more articulate expression of your existence. So may you create and leave a legacy with the intention of knowing your birthright and intuitive self.

You are always invited to return to any of these rites of passage and do them again or as a birthday or anniversary ritual. As you know, rites of passage are not stagnant if we are alive; we are always invited to bring intention to each act.

Thank you for taking this journey yourself and risking living in your glory. I am grateful for women who will not turn away from their authentic lives, because this world is only made better when we live in full glory.

May you always look at her reflection differently.
May you know that she bears the knowledge of love, loss, and hope in her story.

May you know her rites.

Acknowledgments

This book would not have been possible without the support and input from countless people. I am so grateful to you all.

Dr. Andrew Bauman, for lying down next to me every night faithfully because you see the most jagged edges of me that no one else sees. My children, beloveds, you challenge my patience and my faith and demand me to love to the fullest. My sisters, my girlfriends, my mothers, my aunts, my grandmothers, and my great-grandmothers . . . you inspired me to understand my rites and the rites of women.

My Little Brie, my Kinz, for your magnificent talent that you bestowed in the artwork of this book.

My agent, Keely, for your belief in my voice and your commitment to my work. Matt, my editor, thank you for your painstaking commitment to editing and getting my words out to the masses.

Memaw, who gave me both my birthright and my legacy, I love you. Bonnie Anne, there is no sister like you, little sister. Thank you for your commitment to my dreams and for editing the words of this book late into the night so we could reach the deadline. My momma, Mary Christine, I love you. Thank you for giving me life. Sending a kiss to your belly button that forever connects me to you. My Jinxy, for going before me and giving me a mentor to look up to. And for letting me use your house as a sanctuary to write this book. To my brother Paul, who reminds me that men can choose to be good and safe. To my sister Lib, for going first because being the oldest requires that of you.

Sparrow, for always pleading that we cannot talk to another unless we have our hands on their heart. You always call me to more. Mel, your consistency requires me to remain until the work is done. Heather, for holding my face to yours even when I want to turn away. Steph, your friendship requires me to keep a heart that bleeds for relational justice. Alyssa, for letting me bless you and curse you while you coach me as I labor through this life. Cherie, for the light in your eyes that keeps my wonder alive. Autumn, even when it is costly, for praying and fasting on my behalf. Rebecca, for the gift of quick friendship.

Jordan, my Jordie, for all the meals and kitchen conversations. Wren, Aelah, Maddy, Jaci, and Kelsey: the bodyworkers who have cared for my body through this process. All of me is grateful for all of you. Tracy, a sage-femme to me, for making me leave the Red Tent, and promising to be there when I return. Cathy, because you have a fierce determination for friendship. Hayden, because you see me, and I feel it. Nicole, my ride-or-die, who shoots it straight. Nanny Shirlene, thank you for how you continue to lead with grace and love. Nanny Janet, who helped me understand the rite of initiation.

To all the men, guy friends, and mentors: Dan Allender, Jim Coffield, Andrew Bauman, Kirk Boone, Chris Bruno, Sam Jolman, Scott Gibson, Jay Stringer, Brandon Cook, Adam Young, Justin Williams, Ian Vidrine-Isbell, Gary Paine, "Pop" Mike Anthony, Dr. John Paul Isbell, Pastor Andy Carlson, Pierre Vidrine, Steve Kroeger, Colton Winger, Bryan Tucker, Billy Smith, Ben Katt, and Brandon Berry, who have grown weary of women's silence and long for our wholeness.

To all the females I have had the honor of sitting with in therapy, mentors, and sage-femmes who light the way: Pastor

Hayden Wartes, Emilie Townes, Angela Tucker, Dr. Brenda McNeil, Rose Swetman, Patsy Briggs, The Barefoot Preacher Magnano, Becky Allender, Karen Schneider, Shannon K. Evans, Dr. Brené Brown, Rev. Elizabeth Roles, Rachel Clifton, Delores S. Williams, Austin Channing Brown, Dr. Tina Schermer Sellers, Clarissa Pinkola Estés, Renee Trudeau, Dr. Vanya Leilani, and Dr. Katie Douglass.

To Sarah Siskind, Jane Kramer, Emily Mills, and all the musicians who worked on lyrics and music for the *Her Rites* album.

Thanks to Dara for editing this book and believing in this work for women everywhere.

To Convergent, for being a beacon that shines as a guidepost through difference and controversy with the belief that love wins and all will be well. Thank you for carving a path in Christianity for platforms seeking diversity and honest conversations. To all the artists, designers, marketing, and production teams at Convergent, I am so grateful for the work you do in this world and did on behalf of *Her Rites*.

To all the women in the world, who make me damn proud to call myself a woman. May we continue in this work of wholeness to fully know Her Rites.

HER RITES
Marking Guides

Marking Your Rites of Passage

"There are some things we cannot experience without ritual," argues social anthropologist Mary Douglas. Ritual is a buzzword these days, yet it often still intimidates people, and in the religious context, it's especially intimidating to Christians outside of liturgical traditions like Catholicism. As my husband, Andrew, would say to me, "Honey, don't get too woo-woo—Christians won't read it." Don't worry, I am not asking you to get crazy. However, reading a book is *not* the same as performing a ritual. You can read this whole book and answer all the questions, but there is something unique and transformative that happens when we take action. Academic research has demonstrated this reality. One notable example is Jack Mezirow's work, known as transformative learning theory, which has shown that learners (in this case, you and I) experience transformation when they put meaning with an experience.

In my own story, losing my son was a traumatic event I spent years working through psychologically. But even before the psychological work, my grief invited me on a physical journey: a pilgrimage. After my son's death, I took a physical pilgrimage to Southeast Asia and spent months with children who had lost their parents, because I was a parent who had lost my child. That physical journey marked my story with my son within me.

Phil Cousineau discusses the journey of marking transformative work in his book *The Art of Pilgrimage*. He defines pilgrimage as "a transformative journey to a sacred center," which invites individuals to mark their psychological journey with a physical and spiritual one. Marking one's rites of passage can be done in any fashion as long as it is done with intentionality. As the Taoist ritualist Martin Palmer says, "True pilgrimage changes lives, whether we go halfway around the world or out to our own backyards."

In this book, at the end of each rite of passage, there are guided steps that you can use as a template for creating your own ritual. Here are some steps to consider as you work through the rites of passage and decide on rituals to mark them:

+ Journal: Recall the stories. Write them down.
+ Preparation: Deliberately set aside time to consider what elements, space, and objects you want to make use of in a marking ritual. Take your time and wait in quiet areas as you brainstorm ideas. Space is important, and making sure you don't feel rushed and that you feel safe is how you'll make space to be inspired.
+ Meaning making: Be deliberate about making meaning. Take time to imagine surroundings intentionally to facilitate the mood and space. The physical place is essential: topography, climate, or season. Some people might build an ebenezer from river rocks, a firepit from stone, a labyrinth path of logs, or an archway from vines and flowers. Some women might want to do a ritual at a particular body of water, a cemetery, or even the address of their childhood home, school, or college, depending on what is being marked.
+ Word: Writing out the flow of the ritual by beginning, middle, and end. Remember, you can use poetry, writings, songs, silence, a word as these parts of the intentional time. Also, repetition is important. For example, doing things in threes

or sixes is common to incorporate repetitiveness for the human psyche to catch on to and to build a deeper groove in your brain.

✦ Create or purchase items for the time: art, objects, images, prints, macramé, pictures. Sacred objects have long been used by the church to signify meaning: a chalice for water or wine; a glass bottle for oil; a paten, ciborium, or pyx to hold bread; even a monstrance to display collected ash or dirt from a sacred time.

✦ Respect whatever you create as your way of marking: When we use our hands to create, we must respect there is a held sacredness in each item because it holds our time, intention, and talent.

✦ Reflect: Is this something you want to do alone or with others? Often we want to invite a few people to bear witness to our intention. Other times, we know we must do it alone and attest only to ourselves. There is no right or wrong. For myself, there have been times when I do a ritual alone, and then ask my partner or friends to join and I re-create it.

After you have worked through these plans, invite a friend to join you in putting the ceremony into action. Even if you do the ritual alone, it is okay to ask for a friend or others in your community to help you plan the time. There is a marking box that is available to purchase with this book that will accompany you through each rite of passage. I have also listed resources on my website (www.christybauman.com) that connect you to ritual guides.

BIRTHRIGHT
Marking Guides

How to Use the Birthright Guide

Are you ready to claim or reclaim your birthright?

IF YOU FEEL READY TO stake your claim as one who belongs in this world and you are prepared to begin exploring who you are and who you are becoming, then set about to celebrate this rite of passage. You might tell trusted friends or family you want to hold a birthright ceremony. Following the guide below, prepare yourself and your community for the ceremony. Then, mark this passage so you can step into yourself more fully and allow others to see you. Some ideas to consider incorporating into the birthright ceremony: keeping it to about fifteen to twenty minutes, writing an inviting opening to commence by speaking your name, reading your writings, marking your physical body or clothing with elements, and, finally, asking others to speak at the end of the ceremony.

Birthright Template

If you need more structure to help you reclaim your birthright, you can use this template as a guide to awaken your imagination and spirit. There are many ways this can be done, and this is a straightforward example to help you begin to reclaim your own story and give a new narrative to share with those whom you are in a relationship with. Take the time to fill this one out or write your variation of this birthright. Some people also write out the timeline of their actual day of birth and use this as a guide to creating their birthright. Let your creative mind lead you to create a birthright that feels honest to you rather than making it about what anyone else will think.

Legal Name:

Birthright Name (new name one is claiming):

Poem Template to be written and read.

My name is _____ but I was originally
                 (BIRTHRIGHT NAME)

given the name _____.
                        (LEGAL NAME)

I am _____; I came into this world
(ADJECTIVE DESCRIBING YOU)

through a relationship of _____
(ADJECTIVE DESCRIBING YOUR MOTHER)

and _____. Before my first cry of
(ADJECTIVE DESCRIBING YOUR FATHER)

life, my body grew inside of a place of _____
(HOPEFUL VERB OR NOUN)

and _____. As she grew, she beat all
(COMPLEX VERB OR NOUN)

odds of death, she only knew her goodness.

In the womb, I was given _____ hair,
(ADJECTIVE AND COLOR)

_____ eyes, and a
(COLOR AND ADJECTIVE)

_____ body. When I followed the
(ADJECTIVE OR ADVERB)

light, I found myself.

I heard her rage for breath, and she was magnificent. Glory

wanted _____ for me,
(WORD OR PHRASE)

and evil wanted _____.
(WORD OR PHRASE)

I will live out my birthright, the world will know that I am

_____.
(BIRTHRIGHT NAME OR BIRTHRIGHT PHRASE)

A Marking Guide for Birthright

+ Birthright is a right, privilege, or possession to which a person is entitled by birth. By claiming your birthright, you are claiming your right to belong in this world.
+ Use the writing template below to work through your birth story and write out a birthright ritual, such as a baptismal piece to be read during your birthright ceremony. Writings for the birthright ritual should address

+ Who one is as a child of their Creator God
+ The family lineage that the birthright is derived from
+ First, middle, or last names that share intentional meaning

+ Create a shield, crest, or art piece that symbolizes your birthright. Multiple components, such as four quadrants on a crest or shield, often exist. The birthright usually includes words, images, or phrases from the individual's ethnic and family cultural history, birth story (such as place of birth, type of birth, etc.), and/or attachment style with the caregiver. It can hold multiple meanings, such as spiritual names or heritage from God.
+ Elements that one might consider using as marking tools during the birthright ceremony:

    + Water—use this element for cleansing, washing, or baptizing

✦ Essential Oil—use this for smell, anointing, or diffusing
✦ Ash—use ash to mark the body for grief or spread ash in a sacred place or over a body of water, or in a creek
✦ Gold Dust—use this element to mark beauty, glory, or resurrection
✦ Cloth or Sarong—use this to wrap oneself in, lay it on the ground to sit on, hold and smell the item
✦ Jewelry or Christening Item—place in a specific area or hold in your hand during the ceremony

✦ Closing prayer to be read over the individual receiving or claiming the birthright:

> *(Birth name), you come from (family name),*
> *You are a child of the Most High,*
> *Who has called you Beloved,*
> *You belong to this body you've been bestowed,*
> *You are worthy of this life you have been given.*

How to Use the Birthday Guide

A birthday gets more complex as I age, my emotions get confusing, and I often don't know how to celebrate or mark this important day. This guide is created for you to reflect on this year's birthday so that your body might have a chance to share what you are feeling inside in this year of life. There is a birthday writing example and template for you to use as an invitation to create your own.

Birthday Writing Example

Forty-one years ago today, I came into the world before anyone expected me. I was wide-eyed and curious about this world. I was hungry to live from the very beginning. My mother was exhausted, but my grandmother was alert and focused. Roses were wrapped around my momma's hospital bed as she pushed me into this world. I cried for oxygen and then fell quiet, my brown, saucerlike eyes taking in the faces around me. My grandmother's words were that sometimes the hardest to get here are the biggest blessings. My mother took me in her arms and spoke my birthright over me: "You will be my daughter of joy." I have lived so many years since that moment. I have survived death and gone around the sun forty-one times now. I am every age I have ever been, and

I am forty-one years old today. I will be with all of me, recognize that she has seen more than she should have and still longs for more. I am satisfied that I will never be satisfied, and with whatever life I am allowed, I intend to astonish you all.

Birthday Template

_____ years ago today, I came into the world
(YOUR AGE)

_____.
              (DESCRIPTION OF YOUR ARRIVAL)

I was _____-_____ about this world.
        (TWO-WORD DESCRIPTIVE ADJECTIVE)

I was _____ from
     (ADJECTIVE ABOUT YOURSELF ON YOUR DAY OF BIRTH)

the beginning. My mother was _____;
                             (KIND NAMING OF YOURSELF)
                             (DESCRIPTIVE WORD)

she was _____
        (FINISH THE STATEMENT BY DESCRIBING YOUR MOTHER'S

_____.
        LIFE AT THAT TIME OF YOUR BIRTH)

_____ was there
(ANOTHER PERSON PRESENT ON YOUR DAY OF BIRTH)

and she/he was_____.
              (DESCRIPTION OF THEIR PRESENCE IN YOUR LIFE)

The story of my birth is retold with these words:

_____, _____, _____, _____.
(WRITE A DESCRIPTIVE SENTENCE WITH ANY DETAILS OF YOUR
PRESENCE, YOUR BIRTH SURROUNDINGS, OR YOUR TEMPERAMENT)

My skin was _____, my eyes were _____, the
(TINT/SHADE DESCRIPTION)   (COLOR/TINT)

color of _____.
(INANIMATE OBJECT OR A PERSON)

My birthright could be made up of these words: _____

_____.
(CREATE A BIRTHRIGHT STATEMENT OF BELIEF FOR YOUR LIFE)

I inherited _____ on my day of birth.
(NOUN OR DESCRIPTIVE VERB)

I have lived so many years since that moment. I am so much

less _____ than that time, and I have
(A NEGATIVE TRAIT)

become so much more _____ now.
(A POSITIVE TRAIT)

I have survived _____ years and walked
(A HARD MOMENT/S IN YOUR LIFE)

around the sun _____ times now.
(NUMBER OF YEARS)

I am every age I have ever been, and I am ____, ____, and ____
(AGE YOU ENJOYED, DISLIKED, AND ARE)

years old at once.

I will be with all of me, recognize that she has seen

_____ and wants you to know
(VERB OR PHRASE)

that she _____.
(A STATEMENT OF INTENTION)

Happy day of birth to you, _____, I am
(YOUR NAME)

so grateful you are _____.
(SUMMARIZING AND DESCRIPTIVE PHRASE)

A Marking Guide for a Birthday

✦ If spending the day alone, choose a place that reminds you of your most known self. Elements can be helpful, such as swimming in a body of water, reading by a fire, or movement in the wind. There also may be a place such as a mountain-top, an ice cream shop, or a body of water that you can travel to on your birthday.

✦ If you are celebrating with others, be clear with them and with yourself about why their presence at your birthday matters to you. Invite friends and ask them to bring words, a poem, an image, or a gift that reminds them of you.

✦ Prepare, order, or have friends bring dishes that are impor-tant to you at the gathering and remind you of the celebra-tion. The European tradition on birthdays is to have the one celebrating a birthday cook their favorite meal for their friends. Use some spin-off of this idea with the food you choose to have to be significant to you.

✦ Some ideas to consider are

> ✦ Piñatas, music DJ, created playlist, interpretive dance, or lip sync
> ✦ Spoken word, ritual, or toasts given by others in honor of the birthday person
> ✦ Games, celebration, jokes, and humor as entertainment for the day

✦ Enjoy being celebrated and read a piece written about your birthday or year lived

✦ Close and say together in unison:

Happy day of birth, good _____.
(NAME)

We celebrate your life in this world.
Happy, happy birthday, good woman.

INITIATION
Marking Guides

How to Use the Initiation Guide

Now it is your turn; this is the time to tell your rite of womanhood, your coming-of-age stories. While you may have had a bat mitzvah or a quinceañera, a tradition of initiation is similar, but much more frequent than a onetime event. Remember, initiation is when you cross the threshold into something new, the first time you parent yourself without someone there to parent you. Collect these stories in your mind and write them down. Look through old photos and memory boxes and remember how your coming of age unfolded. A girl slowly becomes an experienced woman through events such as having her period, holding someone's hand, kissing, or having sexual encounters. Rites of initiation are not just in the past but are happening all the time. They are a part of living in a new era or situation in which you are no longer naïve and now know something you didn't before. So let's mark it.

I will use a woman's menstrual cycle as an example of initiation. Every twenty-eight-day cycle is a deeper initiation into a stage of life. We know that a woman's uterus has a lifespan that includes three stages: adolescing, which means to grow up; reproduction, which is the time the eggs prime for fertilization; and senescing, the growing down, or hormonally falling asleep. Within these three stages, our period continues to cycle through: the menstrual, follicular, ovulatory, and luteal phases. These phases often correspond with the moon and your body's hormone levels, but they are also likened to the four seasons: spring, summer, fall, and winter. Every month, your body goes through a different season each week. How do we apply this to marking initiation? Let me tell you. The female's uterus is cyclically marking the female body's most creative process—yes, to create a human, but also the female cycle of creation. As women, we can catch the waves of creativity each month when we lean into our hormonal flow. The female body signals when to rest during the fall and winter phases, while creating during the spring and summer phases. In my menstrual cycle, some of my best ideas, songs, or book-writing sessions happen when I am on my period. In marking my menstrual cycle, I have learned that setting aside one or two nights every time I am on my period is very produc-tive for writing. Often, I make a good pot of tea, get into cozy pajamas, and head upstairs to our guest room, where I write songs or stories late into the night.

Marking your rite of initiation can be done by reflecting on your cycle. If you want to, remember the first time you started your period and write out that story. Or you can notice each week of your cycle, your mood, or your energy level during the different phases of the "seasons." Notice when you want to crawl into bed and watch Netflix, or when you feel like running or swimming: your body is telling you something. Make notes when you feel inspiration and mental excitement. The female body can lead you to understand your creative process. We can mark our period by creating a ritual of marking each menstrual cycle. The week before my period, I try to get a massage, and the week after my period, I often try to go to a bathhouse or spa. These are just some ways to mark the rite of passage through your menstrual cycle.

Initiation is my favorite rite of passage to mark because it can be done repeatedly, depending on how often you need to embody it. Because we are ever-growing creatures, we are often invited into the rite of initiation; we can go from unknowing to knowing. Even if you do not want to mark a cycle monthly, you can do something annually to bring awareness to your body's aging. For example, I go to a Korean spa for the day multiple times a year to continue healthy body image work in my own story. It becomes a way to slow down and let my body know I see its bravery. While I cold-plunge or detox in a steam room, the spa environment helps me let my body know that I remember its story of moving from naïvete to experience. Sometimes I go alone, other times I go with friends.

Another cyclical touchstone to mark is sexuality. When it comes to sexuality, in particular, we must begin with sensuality. Sensuality is inviting each sense: touch, taste, smell, sound, and sight. Guiding oneself through initiation is to engage in our senses and awaken them to the present. Here are a few examples of how one can do that.

✦ If you are on your period, choose a night to pamper yourself: draw a warm bath, prepare a special drink, get into cozy pajamas, and bring a journal, a good book, or a fun movie.

✦ Find a Korean spa or similar spa where you can fully immerse your body in different temperatures of water and bathing areas. Plan to spend a few hours; bring your journal, a good book, and intentional tools to help you feel embodied.

✦ Cook a meal you have never cooked before—whether trying to cook a meal from another culture or something on your own, prepare a dish you have never made. Buy a cookbook, ask a family member, google a cultural dish, and choose something new that you want to try.

✦ Initiate a movie night centered around girls becoming women—pick themes about rites of passage such as first loves, menstruation, and sexual awareness. Use this time with other friends, nieces, and daughters—marking the stereotypical act of a girl's initiation into womanhood. Celebrate being a woman by having intentional conversations after the movie.

✦ Some movies to consider for this time:

    ✦ *Pad Man*
    ✦ *Turning Red*
    ✦ *To All the Boys I've Loved Before*
    ✦ *The Summer I Turned Pretty*

Initiation Template

When my kids started memorizing poems, Marianne Wil-
liamson or Rudyard Kipling quotes could be heard at different volumes around our house. Statements were said when
I least expected them: "Our deepest fear is that we are
powerful beyond measure" or "Or walk with kings—nor lose
the common touch." One day on our way to a Juneteenth
rally, my son screamed, "Our presence automatically liberates
others!"

These examples are about recognizing phrases that initiate
us into the task before us. It is like a pep talk we give ourselves when we need to get hyped for an event. For example,
after I finished my book *Theology of the Womb*, I was driving
to my first book event. I had spent months working on the
concept of the life-death-life cycle. It isn't surprising that on
the drive to this event, I hit a deer. As my headlights zeroed
in on the deer's white underbelly, I clipped it and yelled, "For
something to live, something must die!" Few of us know with
such clarity what we believe, until we are posed with a life-
threatening moment, and we yell out. This was my most authentic belief and fear: "For something to live, something must
die."

I want you to write your own phrases or poems to your most
authentic self. Call forth to the person inside of you that needs

the courage to step fully into this next season. The rite of initiation is just that, a moment of crossing over. Would you consider giving yourself some mantra or poem to mark this rite? Feel welcome to write freehand using a poet's words to inspire you or the Mad-Libs-style template below.

A Marking Guide for Initiation

I am not afraid of my _____ anymore,

she was exactly who she needed to be before now,

_____ and _____.

My naïvete will be kindly recalled as _____

_____.

The moment I walked through the gauntlet of _____

_____ and _____,

I saw that she was actually _____

and even more _____

than I realized.

Now I will look at her more clearly, as one who is

_____.

For I have been initiated, now I come to the world

_____ and _____.
(TERMS SUCH AS KNOWING, AWARE, CLEAR, ETC.)

My presence will offer others more than I have ever before. I

stand before me now, more of who I can be, becoming this

woman I call me.

EXILE
Marking Guides

How to Use the Exile Guide

In exile, we go through stages of grief. First, we feel denial, then anger; we bargain, and then the depression sets in. Finally, we come to acceptance. We spend a lot of time in our minds during exile. It is helpful to do our most introspective work during exile. We must come to identify the inner voices we hear when we are alone with ourselves and to whom those voices belong.

When I am alone with my reflection, I often hear the voices of the men in my family who commented on my body shape. I critique the body parts that do not adhere to the patriarchal standard. For example, my grandfather always reminded me that five to ten extra pounds make a big difference in my body type. While I can try to see that he was attempting to "help me out" by letting me know this, the words ring in my head whenever I am alone with my reflection. I more easily bless the seasons, am more physically toned, and challenge myself to lose weight in the seasons when I am more than ten pounds over my ideal weight.

Our internal voices aren't always about our physical bodies; they can also be about our accomplishments or perceived lack thereof. Maybe we hear the assaults of parents who are disappointed in the choices we made in our lives: whether we went to college or pursued a different path, maybe we chose a partner they didn't approve of or had children or not. These accusations should not have authority over our belief system. When we have completed the rite of exile, we have the gift of our authentic voice—the things we tell ourselves are the truest.

It is important to identify what phrases you hear and identify the person who spoke those to you while you are in the rite of exile.

Exile Template

These are the phrases I hear when I am alone and in the rite of exile. Fill in any that apply.

_____

—words my mother said to me.

_____

—words my father said to me.

_____

—words my sibling said to me.

_____

—words my friend said to me.

_____

—words my maternal grandmother said to me.

_____

—words my maternal grandfather said to me.

_____

—words my paternal grandmother said to me.

_____

—words my paternal grandfather said to me.

_____

—words my in-laws said to me.

A Marking Guide for Exile

When you are coming out of a season of exile, the bravest move is to reenter with intention. Whether you have just survived the loss of a loved one, severed a close relationship, or made a difficult transition into a new place—when exile is over, we must reenter with integrity. Our newfound peace with exile can often make us reluctant to share with others, once we have returned, these intimate stories of our time away in the desert.

Over time, look for an item of jewelry, a tattoo image, or a piercing that signifies to your body your time in exile.

Invite others whom you would like to intentionally share with what your season of exile was like. Gather in a circle, around a fire, or a deliberately set table—share with these chosen people what your season of exile entailed. Offer them some of your journal writings and share some of the phrases you heard in your mind. Also, tell them what your most authentic voice sounds like and explain how you can distinguish between others' voices and your own authentic voice. Show them what token (jewelry, tattoo, piercing, etc.) you chose to symbolize what that season was like to your body.

Ask others to share about seasons of their lives when they experienced exile.

CREATION
Marking Guides

Creating Questionnaire

Use the questions to look for a theme to the way you like to create.

1. What is the first thing you think of when you wake up?
   What I have to do today
   What I dreamed about
   What I love or wish I was doing (passion)

2. If you dream, what does it usually consist of?
   What I watched on TV last night
   Another person (lover, friend, etc.)
   Myself—I am alone in the dream or I am the main character

3. What element makes me most intrigued?
   Water, Mountain, Land, Fire

4. In categories borrowed from therapist Dan Allender, I consider myself:
   Prophet/prophetess
   Priest/priestess
   King/queen

5. Do you enjoy speaking, performing, singing, or building? Put these in order of what you enjoy most when you are alone:

Singing—writing songs or playing an instrument
Movement—playing, sports, dance, free-form movement
Building—drawing, constructing, creating
Writing—poetry, blogs, books, stories

6. What season of your life are you in?
Growing/adolescing: 0–30
Creating/reproduction: 30–60
Menopause/senescing: 60–90

A Marking Guide for Creating

Marking the rite of creating is such an untamed time. Creating is such a fluid act that can become anything when given space, tools, and other opportunities. Creating can involve whatever tools help you get into a creative space. Where do you feel most creative? In nature, with a blank canvas, in a room full of instruments, or with a laptop—these are just a few ideas of spaces where you might feel your creativity flow.

✦ Rent a place for the weekend in your favorite topography: mountains, ocean, farmland, island, wooded cabin, desert yurt, downtown hotel, or boathouse.

✦ Pack food, water, and art supplies or writing journal and take a special hike in the terrain of your choice—make sure you plan to watch a sunrise or sunset during your time for creative reflection.

✦ Take a course or class training you in whatever you are interested in: pottery, sailing, painting, memoir writing, sewing, mountain biking, music, or voice lessons.

INTUITION
Marking Guides

How to Use the Intuition Guide

Directions: Describe your journey of the intuition rite of passage. You can write this in your own way or use this template to guide you to articulate the process you have undergone. This poem can be read aloud during the intuition ceremony. Here is an example of the poem after the template has been filled in. Use this example to help you explore ways of creating your poetry.

My prose template to help you be creative with the exercise.
As a young girl, my sister told me my one beauty was my long curly hair. My eyes were made fun of as "poopoo" brown. I believed myself to be valued only by the wit of my words and the beauty of my body. As I grew older, I stared at my reflection until I saw through the curses others brought upon me. Who I knew myself to be offered a road map of my story. She renamed my brown eyes the perfect gumbo roux color, a metaphor that anchors my lineage in the steady hands of my mother's stirring in the kitchen. My inner child proved to me she loves basketball, the color purple, and swinging hard and high on swing sets in the rain. My future self has brilliant silver-guitar-string hair, and when she walks, the wind plays songs that many are intrigued by and comforted by. She has always been called Phoenix Beauty and will guide me to call forth all that is beautiful to emerge from the ashes.

Historically, I have seen myself as _____

(DESCRIPTIVE ADJECTIVES, HOW YOU SAW YOURSELF

and _____, but I now can see that

WHEN YOU WERE YOUNGER)

she is _____ and _____.

(DESCRIPTIVE ADJECTIVES ABOUT HOW YOU SAW YOURSELF IN THE FUTURE)

She knew herself as a young soul, free to live with a

_____ and aware of

(WORD/S DESCRIBING YOUR INNER CHILD)

what is _____.

(SUPPORTING PHRASE TO THE DESCRIPTIVE WORD)

My inner child has shown me she has always been

_____ and the sage-femme

(A KIND, AFFIRMING DESCRIPTION)

inside myself leads me to offer my _____

(A POSITIVE ATTRIBUTE ABOUT YOUR FUTURE SELF)

to the world.

I name my intuitive self _____, and

(A NEW WILD NAME FOR YOURSELF)

she will guide me as I continue to move in this world.

A Marking Guide for Intuition

✦ The ceremony to mark a rite of passage around intuition should occur in a secluded place; the one marking might hire a massage therapist or bodyworker to come and give her a massage. This ceremony should be done alone and allow only yourself to bear witness to your tradition of letting go of the old and integrating deeper into yourself.

✦ Before the actual massage and ceremony, you should prepare by walking through a market and choosing food to create a charcuterie board that signifies a balance of pairings you love. Choose food items that are significant to you, such as a mixture of cheese, nuts, meat, fruits, or dipping sauces that originate from your homeland or places of particular origin to one's heritage.

✦ Consider going to an apothecary or a boutique shop and purchasing a few items that feel significant to your body.

  ✦ Essential oils, lotions, rose water, blessed water, or oils
  ✦ Pink salts, palo santo or white sage, selenium, or other precious stones
  ✦ Write out phrases, verses, poems, or any words on pieces of paper
  ✦ Macramé, yarn, string, and sticks (creating a macramé piece or a God's eye)

✦ Write words such as a poem or story of your intuitive nature.
✦ Bring the fruit and other foods you bought at the market, candles/fire, your writings, and items you have purchased. After the massage, find a quiet, sacred space (usually a place with nature, such as a mountain, seaside, field, stream, or forest) to lay out all your items and mark your intuitive self with an intentional meal.
✦ To end your time, stand and read aloud your words marking your intuitive self.

How to Use the
Where I Come From Guide

Wendell Berry, Elizabeth Brewster, and many womanist theologians have voiced that if you don't recognize where you are from, you will struggle to know who you are and where you are going. Our roots give us the foundation for telling our story and how to articulate our birthright as women. George Ella Lyon's poem "Where I'm From" gives us an image of what it means to name how our culture and history have shaped our knowledge of self. Maybe you have never done this work. I use it with clients and students who haven't penned their past onto paper. There are many templates you can use to create this writing; there are generated templates that help you write your own Where I Come From poem. Feel free to write your own, but you can also use the prompts here to help you dig deep into the recesses of your mind and name your story of roots. Lyon's poem "Where I'm From" inspired this template.

Most women I work with will risk telling me about their birth stories. We will explore the ideas of her father and mother's relationship when she was conceived. We will discuss a rough timeline of her mother's pregnancy and postpartum to understand better the environment in which she entered the world. As we begin mapping out the outline of her early-life narrative, we dig deeper into the culture she was a part of in early childhood. This is the exercise of naming where we come from. You begin to reflect on the home you lived in, the neighborhood, then the town and its culture. Why is this important for you to know? Research shows us that knowing who we start as tells us where we come from. Biblical narratives have also implied the importance of understanding our Christian heritage; we must understand who we are in Christ. The same is true for the physical and psychological just as it is for the spiritual. It is always difficult for clients to look back at their past, sometimes for fear they will never be able to leave it again. Do not fear; I will not leave you in your past.

It was helpful to remember where I came from, reflecting on the tastes, the smells, and the sounds. As I have done each time, I will offer my story and origin to help you explore your own.

✦ Louisiana is my birthplace, a state stocked with Acadian French descendants and rich Cajun heritage. Generations in my bloodline have passed down stories filled with Cajun terminology, ignorance, hunting, and recipes.

✦ Growing up, we spoke Creole French in our kindergarten classroom, and parishes rather than counties demarcate the towns. Napoleonic code influenced Louisiana's legal framework. Traditions, Catholicism, and a vast family gathered around a good gumbo or a crawfish boil are essential to my family tree. I have spent a lifetime immersed in traditions such as Marie Antoinette filling my socks on New Year's or Mardi Gras parades followed by meatless Lent, dyeing eggs for "paq-paq," pronounced "pok-pok," and Easter egg hunts.

✦ School is canceled on the first day of squirrel season, or other unusual events such as skinning and cooking an alligator for family supper, or tanning the hide of your pet deer for taxidermy class.

I also dug into my grandmother's genealogy books. I learned that I come from a group called Acadians, who descended to

Louisiana down the Mississippi River after a brutal exile from Northeastern Nova Scotia. Women and children were banished south and settled in Louisiana, while the men were enslaved for work until they escaped to Louisiana or were killed. Longfellow's famous poem "Evangeline" (1847) captures a small picture of Cajuns' migration to Louisiana from New England. I have stood at Longfellow's "old oak tree" many afternoons and thought about the long-awaited reunions of Cajun families. These stories are the history of the people and my town. Where are you from?

How will you tell your story? The beginning tells us where you came from. What is the culture of the town you come from? In Bronfenbrenner's circle of maturation, we begin by identifying with our family of origin, our family name, and then our childhood neighborhood, the city we are from. It then grows to our home state, our college football team, the continent of the Americas, and finally, we identify as belonging to the Earth. My clients begin by writing a poem about their childhood culture and town. You are invited to do the same: begin to write down aspects of your origins.

Where I Come From Template

We all can benefit from writing about where we come from. The woman who knows who she is can live in her present life, knowing herself better than anyone else knows her. This will allow her to choose to love herself better than anyone else loves her. This act of individuation and self-love is monumental in a woman's health. How she treats herself is a measure of how she can love another. "Love your neighbor as you love yourself" is the second-greatest commandment, after loving God with all your heart, soul, and mind. How will you love God and others? Your answer is evident in how you love yourself. Not in a selfish way, but rather in how you will know the body and story God has allowed you to inhabit. How will you write the story of where you come from? It requires reflecting on your history, family ancestry, and cultural aspects of your origin and childhood environment. Use this template as a writing exercise to pen your story.

I am from _____, from
<small>(A SPECIFIC ITEM FROM YOUR CHILDHOOD HOME)</small>

_____ and _____.
<small>(TWO COMMERCIAL PRODUCTS OR OBJECTS FROM YOUR PAST)</small>

I am from _____
<small>(PHRASE DESCRIBING YOUR CHILDHOOD HOME)</small>

and _____.
<small>(MORE DESCRIPTION OF YOUR CHILDHOOD HOME)</small>

I am from _____ , from
(SPECIFIC, ORDINARY ITEMS)

_____ and _____ .
(SPECIFIC BRAND)   (PRODUCT NAME)

I am from _____ and
(CULTURAL ASPECT)

_____ .
(CULTURAL TRADITION)

I am from _____ and
(A RELIGIOUS MEMORY OR FAMILY TRADITION)

_____ .
(TWO FOODS/THINGS DESCRIBING THAT TRADITION)

I am from _____ and
(A SPECIFIC EVENT IN THE LIFE OF AN ANCESTOR)

_____ .
(ANOTHER DETAIL FROM THE LIFE OF AN ANCESTOR)

I come from the _____ home
(STATE, CITY, OR HOME DESCRIPTION)

of _____ and _____ .
(ADJECTIVE AND SENSORY DETAIL)

I am from the _____ , the
(PLACES, PLANTS, FLOWERS, NATURAL ITEMS)

_____ _____ .
(ADJECTIVE, COLOR, SHAPE)   (PLANT, FRUIT, FLOWER, TREE

I come from _____ and
(FAMILY TRAIT OR TRADITION)

_____ , from
(GENERATIONAL FAMILY NAME)

_____ .
(FAMILY TRAIT OR TRADITION)

I'm from _____,
(PLACE OF BIRTH AND BIRTH ORDER)

_____, and _____.
(COOKING TRADITIONS OR FOOD ITEMS COMMON IN YOUR FAMILY)

I _____ and I am
(SOMETHING YOU WERE TOLD AS A CHILD)

_____.

(FAMILIAR THEME/STORY TOLD ABOUT OR DESCRIBING YOU)

I was born into_____ and _____ and
(DESCRIPTION OF FAMILY ASPECT)   (FAMILY TENDENCY)

_____.

(SPECIFIC FAMILY STORY/DETAIL)

I am from these faces, places, people, and things;

I am _____.
(REPEAT A LINE OR IDEA FROM EARLIER IN THE POEM)

LEGACY
Marking Guides

How to Use the Legacy Guide

Everyone will die. Legacy is the life you live after your physical death. You are to use the legacy guide as a template for mapping out how you want to leave this world and what you want to leave in your absence. To tell a good ending, we must start by telling a good beginning. While your birthright guide helped you navigate some of the first stories, you must now synthesize Where You Come From so that you can write your eulogy and will. Begin by filling out the Where I Come From exercise and then move to the Legacy Marking event.

Legacy Template

This is the life I lived—one of _____
and _____.

Some of the most meaningful moments of my life were:

The time _____
_____.

When _____
_____.

The birthday when _____
_____.

I will never forget the experience of _____
_____.

Some of the people who I loved deeply were _____
_____
_____
_____.

Some of the people who loved me the dearest are _____
_____
_____
_____.

What I hope to be remembered for is _____
_____
_____
_____.

I want the marker of my grave to read _____
_____.

A Marking Guide for Legacy

Gather those who you love and hold a memorial for yourself. Create the type of gathering you would like for your someday funeral. Invite everyone that you want to attend your funeral and write out last words that you would want to say and share with them.

At this point of the book, you know that it is important to be intentional with what is at your legacy marking. Gather photos and videos, writings and journal pieces, and documented moments from your timeline. These things can be a part of the time together. Conduct a toast where you share the things you want to say to those you have invited and let them know ahead of time that you would like them to bring intentional words to share with you.

Much like a wedding reception, you will fashion your own legacy reception. If there are particular things you want to give people, such as inheritance or gifts, this is a great time to bestow them. So many inheritances and wills divide families; it takes integrity to make decisions while you are still alive and let your wishes be known. While you cannot control how you will be remembered, you still have agency over the legacy you leave. This is an invitation to do things differently from the conventional system that divides estates and properties after someone is gone. It is even okay for you to read your will at your legacy marking event.

Sources

INTRODUCTION

Abbey, Elizabeth Anorkor et al. "Dipo Rites of Passage and Psychological Well-being Among Krobo Adolescent Females in Ghana: A Preliminary Study." *The Journal of Black Psychology*, vol. 47, no. 6, SAGE Publications, April 2021, https://doi.org10.1177/0095798421 1011307.

Grebenyuk, E. G. "Rite of Passage and Psychotherapy." *Counseling Psychology and Psychotherapy*, vol. 24, no. 1, Moscow State University of Psychology and Education, 2016, pp. 97–108, https://psyjournals.ru /en/journals/cpp/archive/2016_n1/grebenuk.

Schachter, Michael. *Therapeutics: A Case-based Approach.* World Scientific (Europe), 2025, https://www.worldscientific.com/worldscibooks /10.1142/p574#t=aboutBook.

Van Bavel, Hannelore. "The 'Loita Rite of Passage': An Alternative to the Alternative Rite of Passage?" *SSM—Qualitative Research in Health*, 2021.

RITE OF BIRTH RESOURCES

Farrell, Marinah V. "Why Restoring Birth as Ceremony Can Promote Health Equity." *AMA Journal of Ethics*, vol. 24, no. 4, April 2022, pp. E326–332, https://journalofethics.ama-assn.org/article/why -restoring-birth-ceremony-can-promote-health-equity/2022-04.

Harris, Sarah. "No One Understood Why I Took My Wife's Surname." *The Independent*, August 17, 2008, https://www.independent.co.uk

/news/uk/this-britain/no-one-understood-why-i-took-my-wife-s
-surname-894075.html.

Herron, M. L. *Patronymy as Taken-for-granted and Enforced Patriarchal Practice? Analysis of Marital Naming Practices and Plans*, 2010, https:// digitallibrary.sdsu.edu/islandora/object/sdsu%3A4582.

Hoffnung, Michele. "What's in a Name? Marital Name Choice Revisited." *Sex Roles*, vol. 55, no. 11–12, Springer Science and Business Media LLC, Dec. 2006, pp. 817–825, https://www.researchgate.net /publication/225561837_What's_In_a_Name_Marital_Name _Choice_Revisited.

Schachter. *Therapeutics*.

Shatzman, Celia. "Pregnancy and Birth Traditions around the World." *The Bump*, December 15, 2017, https://www.thebump.com/a/birth -traditions-around-the-world.

The Works of Josephus (William Whiston, trans.). Hendrickson Publishers [First A.D. 93].

Yonatan, T. Genesis 4:1–8. Midrash Bereishit Rabbah, vol. 4, no. 7, 2021, pp. 1–8.

RITE OF INITIATION RESOURCES

Bauman, Christy. *Theology of the Womb: Knowing God Through the Body of a Woman*. Wipf and Stock Publishers, 2018.

Evans, Shannon K. *Feminist Prayers for My Daughter: Powerful Petitions for Every Stage of Her Life*. Brazos Press, 2023.

Koffler, Jacob. "Here Are Places Women Can't Take Their Husband's Name When They Get Married." *Time*, June 2015, https://time.com /3940094/maiden-married-names-countries/.

Lockwood, Penelope et al. "Tampering with Tradition: Rationales Concerning Women's Married Names and Children's Surnames." *Sex Roles*, vol. 65, no. 11–12, Springer Science and Business Media LLC, August 2011, pp. 827–839, https://link.springer.com/article/10.1007 /s11199-011-0034-1.

Mackin, Ellie. "Girls Playing Persephone (in Marriage and Death)." *Mnemosyne*, vol. 71, no. 2, Brill, Feb. 2018, pp. 209–228, https://brill.com/view/journals/mnem/71/2/article-p209_209.xml?language=en.

McLaren, Karla. *The Language of Emotions: What Your Feelings Are Trying to Tell You.* Sounds True, 2010.

Monk Kidd, Sue. *The Dance of the Dissident Daughter.* HarperOne, 1996.

Noack, Turid, and Kenneth Aarskaug Wiik. "Women's Choice of Surname upon Marriage in Norway." *Journal of Marriage and the Family*, vol. 70, no. 2, Wiley, April 2008, pp. 507–518, https://onlinelibrary.wiley.com/doi/abs/10.1111/j.1741-3737.2008.00497.x.

Nelson, Elizabeth Eowyn. "Embodying Persephone's Desire: Authentic Movement and Underworld Transformation." *Journal of Jungian Scholarly Studies*, vol. 11, University of Alberta Libraries, June 2016, pp. 5–17, https://jungianjournal.ca/index.php/jjss/article/view/37.

Norris, Rebecca. "15 Famous Women Throughout History and Their Lasting Impact." *Woman's Day*, January 27, 2023, https://www.womansday.com/life/g42642115/famous-women/.

Pretchel, Martin. *The Smell of Rain on Dust: Grief and Praise.* North Atlantic Books, 2015.

Rieuwpassa, Risye Yulika. "Theology of The Womb: Knowing God Through the Body of a Woman." *Jurnal Abdiel: Khazanah Pemikiran Teologi*, vol. 5, no. 2, 2021, pp. 285–292.

Schachter. *Therapeutics.*

RITE OF EXILE RESOURCES

Allender, Dan B., and Cathy Loerzel. *Redeeming Heartache: How Past Suffering Reveals Our True Calling.* Zondervan, 2021.

Brown, Byron. *Soul Without Shame: A Guide to Liberating Yourself from the Judge Within.* Shambhala Publications, 1998.

Sölle, Dorothee, and Joe H. Kirchberger. *Great Women of the Bible in Art and Literature.* Fortress Press, 2006.

Sperling, Jutta Gisela. "Wet Nurses, Midwives, and the Virgin Mary in Tintoretto's Birth of Saint John the Baptist (1563)." *Medieval and Renaissance Lactations*, Routledge, 2016, pp. 235–253, https://www.researchgate.net/publication/286270292_Wet_Nurses_Midwives_and_the_Virgin_Mary_in_Tintoretto's_Birth_of_Saint_John_the_Baptist_1563.

Strelan, Rick. "Elizabeth, Are You Hiding? (Luke 1:24)." *Neotestamentica*. New Testament Society of Southern Africa, 2003, vol. 37, no. 1 (2003), pp. 87–95, https://www.jstor.org/stable/43048459.

"The Holy Family with Saints Elizabeth and John the Baptist." *JAMA: The Journal of the American Medical Association*, vol. 286, no. 24, Dec. 2001, p. 3051, https://jamanetwork.com/journals/jama/article-abstract/194491.

RITE OF CREATION RESOURCES

Bauman. *Theology of the Womb.*

Hou, Chia-Yi. "Chia-Yi Hou." *Business Insider*, https://www.businessinsider.com/author/chia-yi-hou. Accessed August 3, 2023.

Kimmel, Michael S., and Gail Sheehy. "Passages: Predictable Crises of Adult Life." *Contemporary Sociology*, vol. 6, no. 4, SAGE Publications, July 1977, p. 490, https://www.jstor.org/stable/2066478.

Miles, Tiya. *All That She Carried: The Journey of Ashley's Sack, a Black Family Keepsake*. Random House Trade Paperbacks, 2022.

Nugent, Colleen. "Children's Surnames, Moral Dilemmas: Accounting for the Predominance of Fathers' Surnames for Children." *Gender and Society*, vol. 24, no. 4, August 2010, pp. 499–525, https://www.jstor.org/stable/25741194.

Robnett, Rachael D. et al. "Does a Woman's Marital Surname Choice Influence Perceptions of Her Husband? An Analysis Focusing on Gender-Typed Traits and Relationship Power Dynamics." *Sex Roles*, vol. 79, no. 1–2, November 21, 2017, pp. 59–71, https://link.springer.com/article/10.1007/s11199-017-0856-6.

Rogers, Kristen. "Why Women Do or Don't Change Their Name When They Get Married." CNN, July 19, 2022, https://www.cnn.com/2022

/07/19/health/last-name-change-marriage-reasons-wellness/index
.html.

Savage, Maddy. "Why Do Women Still Change Their Names?" BBC,
September 24, 2020, https://www.bbc.com/worklife/article/20200921
-why-do-women-still-change-their-names.

Schachter. *Therapeutics*.

Scheuble, Laurie K. et al. "Married Name Changing Attitudes and
Plans of College Students: Comparing Change Over Time and
Across Regions." *Sex Roles*, vol. 66, no. 3–4, 2012, pp. 282–292,
https://www.ncbi.nlm.nih.gov/pmc/articles/PMC4170063/.

Shafer, Emily Fitzgibbons. "Hillary Rodham Versus Hillary Clinton:
Consequences of Surname Choice in Marriage." *Gender Issues*,
vol. 34, no. 4, Springer Science and Business Media LLC, Dec. 2017,
pp. 316–332, https://www.researchgate.net/publication/312076598
_Hillary_Rodham_Versus_Hillary_Clinton_Consequences_of
_Surname_Choice_in_Marriage.

Stabel, Meredith and Zachary Turpin, editors. *Radicals, Volume 2: Memoir, Essays, and Oratory: Audacious Writings by American Women,
1830–1930*. University of Iowa Press, 2021.

"Statistics on the Purchasing Power of Women." Girlpower Marketing,
May 16, 2017, https://girlpowermarketing.com/statistics-purchasing
-power-women/.

Taylor, Sonya Renee. *The Body Is Not an Apology: The Power of Radical
Self-Love*. Berrett-Koehler Publishers, 2018.

Walker, Alice. *The World Has Changed: Conversations with Alice Walker*.
The New Press, 2010.

RITE OF INTUITION RESOURCES

Buttry, Sharon A., and Daniel L. Buttry. *Daughters of Rizpah: Nonviolence and the Transformation of Trauma*. Cascade Books, 2020.

Crowder, Stephanie Buckhanon. *When Momma Speaks: The Bible and
Motherhood from a Womanist Perspective*. Westminster John Knox
Press, 2016.

Dunn, Betty. "Who Was Rizpah and What Does Her Story Teach Us About the Importance of Grief?" https://www.biblestudytools.com /bible-study/topical-studies/who-was-rizpah.html. Accessed August 3, 2023.

Estés, Clarissa Pinkola. *Women Who Run with the Wolves: Myths and Stories of the Wild Woman Archetype.* Ballantine Books, 1995.

Haleta, Olena. "Joanna the Wife of Chuza by Lesya Ukrainka as a New Model of Communication in Modern Ukrainian Literature [Joanna, żona Chuzy Lesi Ukrainki jako nowy model komunikacji w modernistycznej literaturze ukraińskiej]." *Przestrzenie Teorii,* no. 36, Adam Mickiewicz University Poznan, Dec. 2021, pp. 289–307, https://www.researchgate.net/publication/357291688_Olena_Haleta _Joanna_the_Wife_of_Chuza_by_Lesya_Ukrainka_as_a_New _Model_of_Communication_in_Modern_Ukrainian_Literature _Joanna_zona_Chuzy_Lesi_Ukrainki_jako_nowy_model _komunikacji_w_modernistycznej_lit.

Henderson, J. Frank. *Remembering the Women: Women's Stories from Scripture for Sundays and Festivals.* Liturgy Training Publications, 1999.

Mostafa, Radwa. "Women Accompanying Virgin Mary in Crucifixion Scenes: A Study in the New Testament Scenes." *Journal of Association of Arab Universities for Tourism and Hospitality,* vol. 17, no. 3, October 2020, pp. 1–17, https://jaauth.journals.ekb.eg/article _120109_966caca94cac43130e1e364ca9b19f30.pdf.

Osiek, Carolyn. "The Women at the Tomb: What Are They Doing There?" *HTS Teologiese Studies/Theological Studies,* vol. 53, no. 1/2, December 13, 1997, pp. 103–118.

Rawlings, Deb et al. "Compassionate Communities—What Does This Mean for Roles Such as a Death Doula in End-of-life Care?" *Public Health,* vol. 194, May 2021, pp. 167–169.

Rawlings, Deb, Jennifer Tieman, Lauren Miller-Lewis, and Kate Swetenham. "What Role Do Death Doulas Play in End-of-life Care? A Systematic Review." *Health and Social Care in the Community,* vol. 27, no. 3, September 26, 2018, pp. e82–e94.

Trescott, Jacqueline. "Smithsonian's African American History Museum Acquires Emmett Till Casket." *Washington Post,* August 27, 2009.

Tyson, Timothy B. *The Blood of Emmett Till.* Simon & Schuster, 2017.

Westendorp, Mariske, and Hannah Gould. "Re-feminizing Death: Gender, Spirituality and Death Care in the Anthropocene." *Religions* 12(8), 2021, p. 667. https://doi.org/10.3390/rel12080667.

RITE OF LEGACY RESOURCES

Albom, Mitch. *Tuesdays with Morrie: An Old Man, a Young Man, and Life's Greatest Lesson.* Crown, 2002.

Alcott, Louisa May. *Louisa May Alcott on Race, Sex, and Slavery.* Northeastern University Press, 1997.

Bhutta, Neil et al. "Disparities in Wealth by Race and Ethnicity in the 2019 Survey of Consumer Finances." 2020, https://www.federal reserve.gov/econres/notes/feds-notes/disparities-in-wealth-by-race -and-ethnicity-in-the-2019-survey-of-consumer-finances-20200928 .html.

Cagnassola, Mary Ellen. "More Americans Are Leaving Inheritances— and It's Not Just Wealthy People." *Money,* April 12, 2023, https:// money.com/more-americans-leaving-inheritances/.

Deen, Edith. *All of the Women of the Bible.* Harper, 1955.

Finch, Janet. "Naming Names: Kinship, Individuality, and Personal Names." *Sociology,* 42, no. 4, August 1, 2008, 709–725.

Hayes, Diana L. *Standing in the Shoes My Mother Made: A Womanist Theology.* Fortress Press, 2010.

"Inheritances by Race," Penn Wharton University of Pennsylvania, Budget Model, December 17, 2021, https://budgetmodel.wharton.upenn .edu/issues/2021/12/17/inheritances-by-race.

Kidd, Sue Monk. *The Book of Longings: A Novel.* Penguin Books, 2021.

Sabelhaus, John Edward and Jeffrey P. Thompson. "Racial Wealth Disparities: Reconsidering the Roles of Human Capital and Inheritance." Federal Reserve Bank of Boston, Working Paper No. 22–3, 2021.

Sheehy, Gail. *New Passages: Mapping Your Life Across Time.* Ballantine Books, 2011.

Suter, Elizabeth A. "Tradition Never Goes Out of Style: The Role of Tradition in Women's Naming Practices." *The Communication Review,* vol. 7, no. 1, January 1, 2004, pp. 57–87.

Wolff, Edward N., and Maury Gittleman. "Inheritances and the Distribution of Wealth, or Whatever Happened to the Great Inheritance Boom?" *The Journal of Economic Inequality,* vol. 12, November 7, 2013, pp. 439–468.

About the Author

CHRISTY ANGELLE BAUMAN, PHD, MDFT, LMHC, is a therapist and professor specializing in Christian women's sexual and spiritual health. She supports women while they work toward self-identity, sexual healing, and hope, and she is committed to helping women come into their authentic voices. She hosts the podcast *Womaneering*, in which she discusses what it means to pioneer a meaningful life.

About the Type

This book was set in Goudy Old Style, a typeface designed by Frederic William Goudy (1865–1947). Goudy began his career as a bookkeeper, but devoted the rest of his life to the pursuit of "recognized quality" in a printing type.

Goudy Old Style was produced in 1914 and was an instant bestseller for the foundry. It has generous curves and smooth, even color. It is regarded as one of Goudy's finest achievements.